THE ROSSMOYNE RENAISSANCE

THE ROSSMOYNE RENAISSANCE

| Aaron Belford Thompson | Priscilla Jane Thompson | Clara Ann Thompson |

Introduction by
Wesley R. Bishop and Patricia Oman

Hastings College Press | Hastings, Nebraska

Harvest of Thoughts © 1907 by Aaron Belford Thompson. *Gleanings of Quiet Hours* © 1907 by Priscilla Jane Thompson. *Songs from the Wayside* © 1908 by Clara Ann Thompson. These books have fallen into the public domain and are no longer subject to copyright protection.

"Introduction" © 2021 by Wesley R. Bishop and Patricia Oman

"Notes on Editing" © 2021 by Patricia Oman

All rights reserved. No part of this book may be used or reproduced in any manner whatsoever without permission from the publisher, except in the case of brief quotations embodied in critical articles and reviews.

Production Staff
Agathe Baume
Max Griffel
Jaidan Hanshaw
Jora Jackson-Brown
Madison Jagels
Ivan Linenberger
Dominica Lotmore
Marcos Montoya
Lilly Nelms
Kyler Samples
Bethany Turner
Charleen Vesin
Jocelyn Wahl
Effy Widdifield

ISBN-13: 978-1-942885-85-6

Introduction	xi
Notes on Editing	lxix

HARVEST OF THOUGHTS

Aaron Belford Thompson

A Bright Reflection	3
A Message	5
Beyond the River	7
Lines to Autumn	9
A Plea to the Muse	12
Night	15
An Ode to Ireland	17
Santa Claus' Sleigh Ride	18
A Christmas Carol	20
Friendship's Parting	21
The Chiming Bells	22
A Proposal	24
A Birthday Tribute	26
Our Girls	28
A Barn-Yard Confusion	29
The Dreary Day	31
To Helen	33
Tale of the Haunted Dell	34
A Deserted Homestead	39
A Serenade	42
Emancipation	44
Miss Susie's Social	46
Boyhood Days	50
The Bachelor's Soliloquy	52

Fritz Mohler's Dream	53
The Same Old Sun	58
Tale of the Wind	61
Reason Why I's Happy	64
Down Murray's Hall	65
The Maiden's Song	70
Life's Procession	72
My Country Home	73
The Foresight	75
Lead Me	78
A Congratulation	79
The Traveler's Dream	82
After the Honeymoon	85
Farewell to Summer	88
Out Among Um	90
Weep Not	95
Quit Yo' Gobblin'!	96
When Johnson's Ban' Comes 'Long	97
Meum et Tuum	101
A Strange Vision	102
Invocation	104
Good-Night	105

GLEANINGS OF QUIET HOURS

Priscilla Jane Thompson

Athelstane	109
The Snow-Flakes	110
The Fugitive	111
Just How It Happened	114

A Prayer	116
Death and Resurrection	117
Adieu, Adieu, Forever	119
The Husband's Return	120
While the Choir Sang	124
Uncle Ike's Holiday	126
A Home Greeting	128
Lines to an Old School-House	129
The Examination	131
A Christmas Ghost	135
A Valentine	138
A Tribute to the Bride and Groom	139
Emancipation	140
To a Deceased Friend	142
An Afternoon Gossip	144
The Muse's Favor	149
The Favorite Slave's Story	152
The Interrupted Reproof	163
Freedom at McNealy's	164
Adown the Heights of Ages	168
After the Quarrel	170
Song of the Moon	172
Insulted	173
Soft Black Eyes	174
Raphael	175
A Domestic Storm	178
A Little Wren	180
In the Valley	181
Address to Ethiopia	183
Autumn	185

Lines to Emma	186
Uncle Jimmie's Yarn	187
Oh, Whence Comes the Gladness?	190
A Kindly Deed	191
The Old Freedman	192
The Old Year	195

SONGS FROM THE WAYSIDE

Clara Ann Thompson

To My Dead Brother	199
Uncle Rube's Defense	200
Memorial Day	201
Johnny's Pet Superstition	203
Hope	205
The Dying Year	206
His Answer	207
Doubt	208
The After-Glow of Pain	209
If Thou Shouldst Return	211
Mrs. Johnson Objects	212
Parted	214
An Opening Service	216
The Christmas Rush	217
An Autumn Day	219
I'll Follow Thee	220
The Easter Light	221
Uncle Rube on the Race Problem	224
Hope Deferred	229
Church Bells	230

She Sent Him Away	233
Out of the Deep	234
Uncle Rube to the Young People	235
The Skeptic	242
A Lullaby	245
The Empty Tomb	246
Drift-Wood	248
Submission	249
The Angel's Message	250
Storm-Beaten	253
The Old and the New	254
Oh List to My Song!	260
Not Dead, But Sleeping	261
The Easter Bonnet	262
Autumn Leaves	264
The Watcher	266

APPENDICES

A. Editing Corrections	269
B. Poems Published in Periodicals	285
C. Complete List of Poems	289

INTRODUCTION

Wesley R. Bishop and Patricia Oman

Clara Ann Thompson (1870–1949), Priscilla Jane Thompson (1871–1942), and Aaron Belford Thompson (1873–1929) were Black midwestern poets who lived and wrote at the turn of the twentieth century.[1] Although their works are known to some scholars of midwestern literature and African American studies, their poems are not easily accessible to general audiences and very little has been written about the poets themselves. We hope this book will bring more mainstream and scholarly attention to the Thompson family poets.

The Thompson siblings' successes in writing and publishing made them part of a rising post–Civil War Black literary arts movement. Together they published a total of seven poetry collections: Aaron's *Morning Songs* (1899), *Echoes of Spring* (1901), and *Harvest of Thoughts* (1907); Priscilla's *Ethiope Lays* (1900) and *Gleanings of Quiet Hours* (1907); and Clara's *Songs from the Wayside* (1908) and *A Garland of Poems* (1926). In addition, Clara published two long poems in pamphlet form ("What Means This Bleating of the Sheep?" (1921 and 1923) and "There Came Wise Men" (1923)), and Aaron published a pamphlet-sized collection of children's poems titled "Rhymes of Childhood" (1924).[2] Except for Clara's last collection, which was published by Christopher Publishing House of Boston, all of their volumes were self-published on Aaron's personal printing press. In their time they received attention from the Black press and were hailed as celebrities in the Cincinnati and Indianapolis Black communities, but, unlike contemporaries such as Paul Laurence Dunbar, they never managed to attain mainstream attention.

We have included in this book Aaron's *Harvest of Thoughts*, Priscilla's *Gleanings of Quiet Hours*, and Clara's *Songs from the*

Wayside, all initially published in 1907–1908, as a snapshot into the artistic and poetic interests of this talented family of poets at a specific moment in early twentieth-century America. Their poetry does not quite follow the narrative scholars have traced for African American literature of this period, the years between the end of Reconstruction (1877) and the beginning of WWI (1917). Rather than mask their voices, as the story goes, the Thompson poets addressed issues of race directly.

The Thompson Family

As the children of formerly enslaved people, Aaron, Priscilla, and Clara did not have an easy path to literary careers. Their parents, John Henry (ca. 1824–1884) and Clara Jane (Gray) Thompson (ca. 1836–1876) were born into slavery in Virginia.[3] They had eleven children: Samuel (1858–1909), Edward (1860–1917), Beverly (1862–1879), Garland (1864–1938), Emma (1867–1878), Clara (1870–1949), Priscilla (1871–1943), Aaron (1873–1929), John (1876–1877), and two additional children who died in infancy.[4] At least four of the older children were born in Kentucky, likely enslaved, though we do not know how or when the Thompson family moved from Virginia to Kentucky.[5] Sometime during or immediately after the Civil War, the family made their way to Rossmoyne, Ohio, a rural neighborhood roughly ten miles northeast of downtown Cincinnati. Rossmoyne was a predominantly white, census-designated area in Sycamore Township, Ohio. Never an officially incorporated town or village, the area was extremely rural when the Thompsons lived there—so rural that the Thompson poets used a P.O. box (Box 17, Rossmoyne) as their mailing address. Today, the area is known as Deer Park, but in records throughout the twentieth century it was also referred to as Blue Ash (a small village located northeast of the Thompsons' farm) and Sharon (a small village located west of the Thompsons' farm). This is where Clara, Priscilla, and Aaron were born and raised.⁶ Clara and Priscilla lived with their brother Garland at the family farm most of their lives.

We do not know exactly how or when the Thompsons came to Rossmoyne. In his 1999 book *The Longest Raid of the Civil War,* Lester V. Horwitz writes that in the 1860s "a black family by the name of N. Thompson" had been smuggled into Ohio by John Schenck, a "conductor" of the Underground Railroad, who "allowed them to use a vacant log cabin and farm the land until the Civil War ended." Drawing on personal correspondence with a granddaughter of John Schenck—Ida Schenck Dittes—for this story, Horwitz further notes that the Thompsons hid themselves on Schenck's farm when the Confederate troops of General John Hunt Morgan stopped there on July 14, 1863.⁷ Based on Horwitz's assertion that "[t]wo of the Thompson daughters went on to become well-known poets of their day," The Ohio Historical Society and the Ohio Civil War Trail Commission identified the enslaved family as the parents of Clara, Priscilla, and Aaron Thompson ("A Famous Family") on a historical marker in front of the Schenck home.⁸ Census records, deed records, and city directories show that the Thompson family did live very close to the Schenck family. In fact, on the census sheet for the 1870 federal census the Thompson family (dwelling 163) is listed directly after the Schenck family (dwelling 162).⁹ Further, the 1910 census shows that as a child Ida Schenck Dittes lived on the same road as the Thompson family.¹⁰ So, theirs is probably the family identified in Horwitz's book.

However, the birth dates and birthplaces of the older Thompson siblings do not quite align with the timeline of this story. The 1870 federal census, for instance, lists Garland's birth year as 1864 and his birthplace as Kentucky. The birth date and place for the next oldest child, Emma, is noted as 1867 in Ohio.¹¹ Given the lack of birth records for enslaved people, there is no way to verify Garland's date and place of birth, but most civil records are consistent on this point.¹² Further confusing the issue is Garland's short biography in Wendell P. Dabney's 1926 book *Cincinnati's Colored Citizens,* which reports that "John Henry and Clara Jane Thompson … came to Cincinnati from Virginia directly after the Civil War and settled in Rossmoyne," apparently bypassing Kentucky.¹³ We estimate, therefore, that the Thompson family arrived in Ohio sometime between 1864 and 1867, which means they likely would not have been hiding in the Schencks' parlor during Morgan's raid in 1863, though it is possible that members of the family arrived in Ohio at different times. Federal census records show that the family was settled in Rossmoyne by 1870.

However the Thompson family got to Rossmoyne, John Henry and Clara Jane worked to improve the family's economic and social status through education and property ownership. The 1870 federal census, for instance, notes that John Henry and Clara Jane could not read or write and only one child (Edward, age 10) had attended school, but the 1880 federal census indicates not only that John Henry could read and write but that Clara (age 11), Priscilla (age 9), and Aaron (age 7) were all attending school.¹⁴ In late 1875 and early 1876, John Henry and Clara Jane bought three adjoining lots of land in Rossmoyne (the address later described as "Plainfield Pike" and "Plainfield Road") for a total of $900.¹⁵ This 5.3 acre property was located just north of the Schenck farm and ran along the diagonal section of Plainfield Road. Unfortunately, this positive step on the economic ladder was followed quickly by a series of tragic deaths for the family. Clara Jane died in May 1876, followed by John (age 1) in December 1877, Emma (age 11) in March 1878, and Beverly (age 17) in May 1879.¹⁶ John Henry died in 1884, leaving Garland—only 20 years old at the time—to care for the siblings still living at the family home: Clara (age 14), Priscilla (age 13), and Aaron (age 11).¹⁷ Despite these tragedies, census records indicate that the mortgage on the farm was paid off by

1920, and the farm stayed in the Thompson family until 1946, when the last remaining sibling, Clara, sold it.[18]

Property ownership continued to be important for the Thompson siblings in adulthood. According to city directories, Aaron moved to 2109 Howard Street in Indianapolis in 1908 or 1909. While the 1910 federal census notes that the Howard Street property was owned but mortgaged, the 1920 federal census lists the property as owned and free of a mortgage.[19] Property ownership was an important detail in a 1912 article on Aaron in Black-run Indianapolis newspaper *The Recorder*, which noted, "During the past few years of success ... the author has not left 'a stone unturned' having purchased a cosy cottage, and erected a snug little publishing house in the rear, he also owns some valuable Real Estate in Ohio near Cincinnati."[20] In 1925 Garland bought a second property in Rossmoyne, 8218 St. Clair Avenue, for $500. Upon his death in 1938, he left it to Priscilla, who in turn upon her death in 1942 left it to Clara. When Clara died in 1949 and left the property to her niece, Emma Smith (Edward's daughter), it was valued at $4,000. According to obituaries, this is the home where Clara died.[21]

The Thompson family seem to have maintained close relations into adulthood. Clara, Priscilla, and Aaron all expressed particular appreciation for their older brother Garland, who was their guardian after their parents died. In fact, all three poets dedicated collections of poetry to him. Aaron's 1901 collection *Echoes of Spring* is dedicated to "My Brother Garland," to whom the author "owes more than he can ever acknowledge or forget."[22] Priscila's first collection *Ethiope Lays* (1900) includes this dedication:

> To him, whose childish hands did smooth
>   My path in infant day,
> And in my riper years, doth soothe
>   My grief and cares away,

> To him, my brother, best beloved,
> From whom I've truth imbibed,
> Dear Garland, friend and warder, proved,
> The firstling is inscribed.²³

And Clara dedicated her 1926 collection *A Garland of Poems* to "my Brother / Garland Yancey Thompson / In Recognition of his unfailing Kindness and Affection."²⁴ In *Cincinnati's Colored Citizens,* Dabney suggests that Garland sacrificed his own ambitions to raise his younger siblings, writing that when his father died Garland had to give up his opportunity to live with and study under "Benjamin Pittman, the noted wood carver, and pioneer expert of stenography of Cincinnati, who encouraged him in the art, and presented him a set of carving tools." Dabney writes further of Garland, "His genius is demonstrated in a rare collection of his handiwork, specimens of which won splendid prizes in the Hamilton County Fair Art Exhibit."²⁵

Wearing the Mask

In their poetry, Aaron, Clara, and Priscilla demonstrate in different, but related, ways the nineteenth-century origins of twenty-first-century cultural politics. The failed dream of Reconstruction created an America tragically out of step with its purported ideals. Lynchings of Black Americans were common in the period when the Thompsons published their poetry collections. In fact, a short article titled "Lynchings of 1906" in the March 1907 issue of *The Colored American Magazine* reported 72 lynchings in the United States in 1906, 65 lynchings in 1905, 87 lynchings in 1904, 104 lynchings in 1903, 96 lynchings in 1902, and 135 lynchings in 1901.²⁶ Many southern states also began instituting Jim Crow laws to segregate Black Americans, seriously curtailing and erasing any progress from the Reconstruction era. The Thompsons were thus writing in a volatile political and social

Garland Yancy Thompson. From Wendell P. Dabney, *Cincinnatti's Colored Citizens* (The Dabney Publishing Company, 1926), p. 316.

moment in American history. Despite an appeal to make post–Civil War America "work" as a racially egalitarian society, many of the Black poets of the period understood that their aspirations for American society were just that—aspirational. In the poetry of the Thompson siblings that tension is visible; their poetry both celebrates the democratic promises of the United States and acknowledges the ongoing failure of white America to live up to those ideals. Furthermore, it places as its hope the experiences of Black Americans.

In some ways, the Thompsons' poetry fits Joan R. Sherman's characterization of Black American literature of the post-Reconstruction period: "Reconstruction sounded the death knell of militant protest poetry and the birth of 'integrationist' and 'upward-bound' types." Largely gone, Sherman argues, were the voices of justified and righteous abolitionists, which were followed by a more genteel voice that worked within American nineteenth-century sensibilities of natural beauty, ideal civil society, and success strategies for Black Americans in the post-slavery United States. "In the last two decades of the [nineteenth] century," she writes, "African-American poets would lower their voices, mask discontents, and write sober, genteel verse largely indistinguishable from their white contemporaries' art. They would portray noble black men and women for the race to emulate and for whites to recognize as capable, responsible citizens worthy of integration into American society."[27] The Thompsons did, in fact, emulate their white contemporaries' art, writing in traditional, rhyming poetic forms and addressing common western themes such as nature, love, and the pastoral. And their poetry incorporates themes of racial uplift. It is not accurate, however, to say that they "lower[ed] their voices" or "mask[ed] discontents." Unlike many of their Black literary contemporaries, the Thompsons, particularly Clara, addressed debates about race directly.

Paul Laurence Dunbar's famous poem "We Wear the Mask" inspired many scholars to adopt the mask metaphor to describe the period between Reconstruction and the Harlem Renaissance as a period when Black Americans tempered their public criticisms of racism.

We Wear the Mask
We wear the mask that grins and lies,
It hides our cheeks and shades our eyes,—
This debt we pay to human guile;
With torn and bleeding heart we smile,
And mouth with myriad subtleties.

Why should the world be over-wise,
In counting all our tears and sighs?
Nay, let them only see us, while
    We wear the mask.

We smile, but, O great Christ, our cries
To thee from tortured souls arise.
We sing, but oh the clay is vile
Beneath our feet, and long the mile;
But let the world dream otherwise,
    We wear the mask!

                    —Paul Laurence Dunbar[28]

Dunbar's poem recognizes both the insincerity and the necessity of the metaphoric mask, but the Thompson siblings took different poetic approaches to wearing it. The similarities among the three collections included in this volume—Aaron's *Harvest of Thoughts* (1907), Priscilla's *Gleanings of Quiet Hours* (1907), and Clara's *Songs from the Wayside* (1908)—suggest that the siblings discussed literature and politics together. That does not mean their poetry is identical, however. While they held similar opinions about the subjects and themes midwestern Black poets should write about, they nevertheless had their own, unique poetic voices.

In 1903, Booker T. Washington published a collection of essays by prominent Black Americans on the topic of *The Negro Problem*. Contributors—who included Washington, W.E.B. DuBois, Charles Chesnutt, and Paul Laurence Dunbar— addressed the ongoing question from the Reconstruction period: Now that slavery is over, how do Black Americans become fully integrated into American culture?[29] This question was a common topic with politicians and public thinkers (white and Black) throughout the last decade of the nineteenth century and the first decade of the twentieth century. Disagreements over the question contributed not only to widespread lynchings and southern Jim Crow laws but also ultimately to the second wave of the Ku Klux Klan in the 1910s and 1920s. *The Colored American Magazine*, which began publication in 1900 and was closely associated with Washington, often hosted essays on this topic during the first decade of the twentieth century, particularly in 1904, when it ran a series of essays called "Industrial Education: Will It Solve the Negro Problem?"[30] Industrial education was Washington's solution to the full enfranchisement of Black Americans into American culture, but others, most notably DuBois, argued that this approach encouraged Black Americans to think too narrowly. While DuBois's thoughts on the subject evolved over his long career, in the early part of the twentieth century he advocated for higher education and argued that the top 10% of Black Americans (the "talented tenth") would serve as leaders.

While they all wrote "genteel" poems, the Thompson siblings also participated in these debates on the "race problem," each in their own way. Aaron, for the most part, avoided overtly political topics in his poems, preferring to focus on entertainment and the common subjects of "genteel" poetry. His position on the "race problem" is nevertheless revealed in poems such as "A Deserted Homestead" (39–41) and the wonderfully ambiguous "Fritz Mohler's Dream" (53–57). Unlike her siblings, Priscilla addressed the history of Black Americans in poems about slavery and delved into the psychology of Black identity, especially that of Black women. Many of her poems examine Black women's roles in promoting middle-class expectations, and some could even be read through a queer lens. Clara was the most politically engaged of the siblings, explicitly calling for social change in poems such as "Uncle Rube on the Race Problem" (224–228). Thus, while the Thompson siblings' poems have many similarities, they also illustrate three different approaches to writing about Black American life in post-Reconstruction America.

Scholars have sometimes written off, ignored, or sidelined the Thompson siblings for other poetic voices, and upon reading their works in the twenty-first century, it is not hard to see why. Their focus on rhyming formal verse and oscillation between Christianity, racial uplift, and socially conservative outlooks make them seem anachronistic compared to the later, more experimental poets of the Harlem Renaissance. But the Thompsons' poems frequently address the lived experiences of Black Americans and force readers to struggle with the legacy of white supremacy in the United States—in doing so, they reveal foundational work for the later New Negro movement and the Harlem Renaissance.

Aaron Belford Thompson

Like Black Arts Movement pioneer Mari Evans (1923–2017), Aaron migrated from his birthplace in Ohio to Indianapolis. He married Luella Dudley in Indianapolis in 1902, settling around 1909 at 2109 Howard Street, in the near west side, where they lived until their deaths—Luella in 1922 from influenza and Aaron in 1929 from a heart attack.[31] Aaron married his second wife, Hallie Words, in 1922.[32] In his initial years in Indianapolis, Aaron worked as a laborer in factories while writing poetry and advertising himself in newspapers as a performer of original poems. Starting sometime in the 1910s, he worked as a printer out of a small shop in his home. One scholar reports that by the time of his death at age 55, "Thompson had suffered from chronic heart disease and rheumatism for many years."[33] This is supported by Aaron's death certificate, which lists "chronic myocarditis" and "chronic rheumatism" as contributing factors in his death.[34] In fact, in *Cincinnati's Colored Citizens,* Dabney notes that Aaron was "greatly handicapped."[35]

We are not sure how to interpret Dabney's assertion that Aaron was "greatly handicapped"—whether this refers to the "chronic rheumatism" and "chronic myocarditis" listed on his death certificate or some other affliction, such as an injury. We are also not sure how long he suffered from this "handicap." A 1907 article in *The Indianapolis Star* describes Aaron as having an "athletic figure,"[36] which suggests he was fairly healthy at this time. He seems to have stopped publishing and giving performances after about 1911, though. In March 1912, *The Recorder*, a Black-run Indianapolis newspaper, ran a story on Aaron announcing a professional comeback after "having been retired from the rostrum for more than a year." The article featured a photo of him in his home office working on verse, preparing performances, and living the life of a man of letters. "As a reciter of his own productions he has no equal," the paper stated. "Possessing as it seems a supernatural tact and individuality which never fails to charm an audience ... Mr. Thompson has consented to fill several engagements the coming spring, and shall probably tour Indiana, Ohio and other adjacent states."[37] We have not found any evidence that Aaron actually undertook this speaking tour, however. And the only publication we can find attributed to him after his 1907 book *Harvest of Thoughts* is a pamphlet of children's poems, "Rhymes of Childhood," published in 1924.[38]

Aaron's three book-length collections—*Morning Songs* (1899), *Echoes of Spring* (1901), and *Harvest of Thoughts* (1907)—deal with a range of issues and topics, such as nature, religion, history, and Black American life. Local and Black newspapers were positive and encouraging about Aaron's poetic ambitions, but scholars have not been so kind. In their 1924 book *An Anthology of Verse by American Negroes,* Newman Ivey White and Walter Clinton Jackson wrote, "Thompson's grammar is somewhat faulty, his diction is poor, and his verse form is almost entirely restricted to quatrains." Their summative assessment of Aaron's first collection, *Morning Songs:* "There are forty poems, badly printed."[39] Similarly, in her 1974 book *Invisible Poets: Afro-Americans in the Nineteenth Century,* Joan R. Sherman writes, "In three volumes, among 100 verses, Aaron Belford Thompson offers very modest evidence of poetic talent. His subjects are conventional.... His versification is trite, and even the simplest iambics prove troublesome."[40]

A brief review of Aaron's first volume, *Morning Songs,* in the December 10, 1899, issue of *The Commercial Tribune* (Cincinnati) is more diplomatic, noting that he is self-taught in both poetry and printing:

> [Aaron Thompson] is entirely self-instructed. He has been discovering the laws of prosody as best he could, and his jingles are remarkably perfect in places. In order to publish his poems, he bought type, set them up and printed them himself.

Instead of complaining about the lack of metrical variety, this review notes, "Mr. Thompson uses simple rhythms, and plays his variations upon the old melodies that have been loved by the people during many ages."[41]

White and Jackson have a point about printer's errors (such as misspelled words and idiosyncratic punctuation) and occasional grammar problems in Aaron's poems. As we explain in the "Notes on Editing" (lxix–lxxxi), this created a dilemma for us in reprinting *Harvest of Thoughts*. However, it is important to emphasize, as *The Commercial Tribune* did, that Aaron seems to have been entirely self-taught. In fact, none of the Thompson siblings would have had any literary career without Aaron's energy and drive. The copyright pages for each of the Thompsons' self-published volumes indicate they were "Printed and for Sale by the Author" or "Published and Sold by the Author." Clues in various newspaper announcements and advertisements reveal that the self-published volumes were all printed on Aaron's printing equipment. A blurb in the "Personal and Society" column of *The Recorder,* for instance, notes, "Miss Priscilla Thompson who has been here [Indianapolis] a few months with her brother A. Thompson has returned to Cincinnati, with her second volume of poems completed."[42] And an advertisement in *The Freeman* tells readers they can buy books by Aaron, Priscilla, and Clara from "The Domestic Publisher," whose address happens to be Aaron's address, 2109 Howard Street, in Indianapolis.[43]

White and Jackson are also correct that Aaron's poems are "almost entirely restricted to quatrains," just as Sherman accurately identifies Aaron's subjects as "conventional." However, these criticisms ignore the fact that Aaron seemed to approach poetry as a primarily aural and performative medium. Many of his poems are written in rhyming quatrains, several in ballad form (the "common meter"). As *The Commercial Tribune* review points out, this reliance on the common meter seems to "show direct influence of noted hymn writers."[44] It is possible that Aaron's understanding of meter developed partly from church hymns or folk music. Newspaper advertisements and notices in Indiana and Ohio in the first decade of the twentieth century also show that Aaron kept a busy schedule of public readings and performances, in contrast to Dabney's assertion that in his later life Aaron was "greatly handicapped." In one advertisement, Aaron billed himself as a "successful Hoosier poet, author, and humorist" who would perform at churches, lodges, and other public gatherings. Furthermore, his advertisement promised, "As a Reciter of his own Productions he has no Equal … He has amused thousands, and can amuse you."[45] In addition to performing, Aaron accepted commissions for poems. In an ad in *The Recorder* from 1903, for instance, "Prof. Aaron B. Thompson, poet and elocutionist" advertised for speaking engagements and "Also Poems written and recited for special occasions."[46]

Ballad form would have been useful in performances. Many of his poems—"Santa Claus' Sleigh Ride" (18–19), for example—are crowd pleasers written for specific occasions or people:

> 'Twas late in the month of December,
>   And all things were merry and gay,
> When Santa Claus came from his dwelling of fame,
>   And took up the [reins] in his sleigh. (lines 1–4)

The version of "Santa Claus' Sleigh Ride" included in *Harvest of Thoughts* is dedicated to "the little ones" (18), but the version in the earlier volume *Echoes of Spring* is dedicated specifically to "my little nieces and nephews."[47] This dedication suggests that the poem was meant specifically for entertainment. The sing-song rhythms of common meter (alternating, rhyming lines of iambic tetrameter and trimeter) lend themselves to easy memory and oral delivery. Further, in the introduction to his second collection, *Echoes of Spring*, Aaron writes that he has "endeavored to comply with the special request of readers, of my firstling, 'Morning

Wanted Engagements

Prof. Aaron B. Thompson, Poet and Elocutionist
is now ready to fulfill engagements at Public Gatherings, Halls and Churchs with a choice selection of his own Works, consisting of

Serious and Comic Poems

satisfaction Guaranteed. Also Poems written and recited for special occasions. Write for Terms and Engagements. Address

728 W. Twelfth Street, Indianapolis, Ind.

Advertisement. *The Recorder,* 17 October 1903.

Why not engage Aaron Belford Thompson, the successful Hoosier Poet, Author and Humorist, who is now Booking Engagements for Churches, Lodges, etc. As a high class Entertainer, Mr. Thompson needs no introduction. And his charming Verses of Various kinds are widely known and highly commended throughout the country. As a Reciter of his own Productions he has no Equal, as a Humorist he Stands second to None He has Amused Thousands, and can amuse you.

Terms Reasonable.   Old Phone, Belmont 326

AARON BELFORD THOMPSON
2109 Howard Street   Indianapolis, Ind.

Advertisement. *The Recorder,* 22 November 1913.

Songs,' by deviating here and there with a love ballad, or a humorous selection."[48] This suggests that Aaron was encouraged to include more entertaining poems among his more serious ones (or at least wanted his readers to believe so).

Although Aaron tried to cultivate an image for himself as a public performer and man of letters, the local white press focused on his day job as a laborer. To celebrate the publication of *Harvest of Thoughts* in 1907 *The Indianapolis Star* ran a full story celebrating the poet and detailing how he worked as a laborer *and* writer—a kind of proletarian poet: "Working as a day laborer in the American Car & Foundry Company's plant in West Indianapolis," the story read, "[Aaron Belford Thompson] has not yet found the leisure time to devote to writing poetry … [I]n the grimy, athletic figure of the young negro in the foundry one would not expect to find a poet. But in his cozy home, seated

Illustrations and photograph, from "Riley Praises Young Negro Poet," *The Indianapolis Star*, 28 July 1907.

at a table covered with manuscripts and surrounded by favorite books, the budding poet is soon discovered."⁴⁹ Accompanying the story was a series of drawings, one showing Aaron working by day at the foundry, the other Aaron working by night at his desk. In between sat a photo of him, showing the dichotomy of Indianapolis's adopted writer.

Aaron was a major figure in the Indianapolis literary scene and was often compared to Paul Laurence Dunbar. Given Dunbar's tragically short life—he died of tuberculosis in 1906 at the age of 33—the media, especially the Black press, wondered if Aaron would be able to assume the position of the leading Black American poet of the United States. "Is Indiana to produce a second Paul Lawrence Dunbar?" *The Indianapolis Star* wondered in its piece on Aaron's publication of *Harvest of Thoughts*.⁵⁰ James Whitcomb Riley made the comparison too when he was asked to review Aaron's work and provide a blurb. "It is gratifying to find so much of real poetic worth in these first published verses of Aaron Belford Thompson," Riley wrote. "Like his racial prototype, Paul Laurence Dunbar, the gifts of Mr. Thompson seem genuinely native, and give high promise of the young poet's literary future."⁵¹ Despite being tokenized as an heir to a "racial prototype" and despite *Harvest of Thoughts* not being his first published verses, Aaron used the endorsement to his advantage, billing himself as

Aaron Belford Thompson, photographed at his home for *The Recorder*, 23 March 1912.

a poet who had been read, reviewed, and recommended by James Whitcomb Riley and in the process forced the reading public to acknowledge that the city was home not only to the likes of Riley and Booth Tarkington, but also to himself.

Poems such as "Out Among Um" (90–94) demonstrate the influence of both Dunbar and Riley. The poem is a more modern, midwestern rewriting of Dunbar's "The Party"—a humorous account of a country party in the South—but written in a dialect similar to the Hoosier dialect made famous by Riley.⁵² The speaker of Dunbar's poem begins,

> Dey had a great big pahty down to Tom's de othah
>   night;
> Was I dah? You bet! I nevah in my life see sich a sight;
> All de folks f'om fou' plantations was invited, an' dey
>   come,
> Dey come troopin' thick ez chillun when dey hyeahs a
>   fife an' drum.

> Evahbody dressed deir fines'—Heish yo' mouf an' git
> away,
> Ain't seen no sich fancy dressin' sense las' quah'tly
> meetin' day; (lines 1–6)

The speaker describes the party-goers' increasingly ridiculous behavior, such as Malindy Jane's "high-toned mannahs" (line 30) and "ole man Johnson," who is "[h]ittin' clost onto a hundred," dancing with three-hundred-pound Aunt Marier (lines 35–40). When poor Scott Thomas falls head-first into the fireplace, the speaker says, "Tried my best to keep f'om laffin', but hit seemed like die I must!" (line 43–54). Aaron's "Out Among Um," whose narrative is structured in the same way as Dunbar's poem, moves the party to a wealthy neighborhood in a northern city. The speaker begins,

> Say boys! you ought 'o been with me,
> Las' night a week ago;
> It won't do you no good to guess,
> Because you does n't know.
> I 'as out among the "Upper Tens,"
> The "Upper Crust," the "Creams";
> Them Tisdales an' the Overstreets,
> The Hunters an' the Jeems. (lines 1–8)

Despite the fact that the party is thrown by the "Upper Tens," DuBois's term for the leading class of Black Americans, it is just as ridiculous as the one described in Dunbar's poem. The speaker describes a mash-up of upper middle-class affectations such as "Sweet cordial nuts and candies" (line 73) and lower-class comfort foods such as "Big yellah sweet potatoes, / Well soaked in 'possum grease" (lines 69–70). The fancy dinner turns to farce when one of the guests, Jackson Jones, tries to gallantly pick up a woman's napkin and ends up spilling a bowl of oyster soup on his head and all over the women around him:

> There were oysters down his collar,
>   An' soup all in his hair;
> His party suit was ruined,
>   I could see it then an' there.
>
> Mrs. Bryant an' the waiters
>   Tried to make the blunder straight;
> I could n't eat another thing
>   That laid upon my plate;
> I was so choked with laughter,
>   I could n't look around;
> An' lookin' solemn in my plate,
>   My face put on a frown. (lines 97–108)

The speaker's response to the funny incident—he "was so choked with laughter, / [he] could n't look around"—is the same as in Dunbar's poem. Also as in Dunbar's poem, it is not clear whether the joke is on the party-goers or the speaker. What is clear is that Aaron has relocated the party to a midwestern city, recast the Black characters as middle-class, and refined the dialect.

Despite his focus on humor and performance, Aaron also tackled serious issues in his poetry. Like his siblings, he viewed slavery as an unforgivable sin that the nation's white population had committed. There was little that could happen in terms of forgiveness, and instead Aaron implies in several poems that the only way for the nation to move on would be to acknowledge the crime. The speaker of "A Deserted Homestead" (39–41), for example, concludes that the ending of slavery had not come from white benevolence but from divine intervention, a supernatural force that had brought judgment down on the American South:

> For the power of that wicked old planter,
>   Who once bound my fathers in chain,
> Had been quelled by the hand of Jehovah,
>   Been severed and broken in twain:
>
> ...
>
> 'Twas the Lord that tore down that dwelling,
>   And checked that old planter's reign;
> Each slave He unyoked from their bondage,
>   And bad them to shake off their chain. (lines 33–56)

What we see here is that despite some literary scholars like Sherman arguing, "Post-Reconstruction poets ... shift[ed] allegiance from a wrathful Jehovah ... to a gentle Jesus," there was still a fair amount of fire and judgment to be had by poets in the post-Reconstruction period.[53] In "The Foresight" (75–77), Aaron even imagines a world in which the racial hierarchy is reversed and "Ethiopia" leads all nations:

> I see Queen Ethiopia,
>   Before all nations stand;
> She is robed in royal purple,
>   And a seal is in her hand.
> As she lifts her hand with jewels,
>   And takes the solemn vow,
> Kings, prince, and nobles hail her,
>   All nations 'fore her bow. (lines 61–68)

"Fritz Mohler's Dream" (53–57) is Aaron's most nuanced poem about the so-called race problem. In this poem, also written in ballad verse, a German immigrant named Fritz Mohler and a Black musician named Scott Johnson have a tense interaction. Mohler watches Johnson perform "old time lively banjo song[s]" (line 27) at a bar on a cold, wintery night but is not amused by the songs, as the other patrons are. In fact, while Johnson plays, "No mirth was in [Mohler's] look" (line 42). All seems well when Mohler insists that Johnson drink with him ... until Mohler describes a "dream" he had in which Johnson stole his chickens. Despite his repeated refrain that "Dot vos a funny thream!" and his repeated insistence that they drink and be merry, Mohler is serious when he accuses Johnson of stealing his chickens. The poem does not reveal whether Johnson actually stole the chickens, leaving readers with an ambiguous and menacing interaction that seems to show a social power play, a German immigrant and a formerly enslaved Black man jockeying for position in America. The faux-joviality of the poem has a thematic parallel to Dunbar's "We Wear the Mask." This is exactly what we see Scott Johnson having to do when he is accused of stealing chickens. In fact, the immigrant Mohler *forces* Johnson to laugh and pretend like the situation is normal. Thus, while Aaron prefers to wear the mask in much of his poetry—focusing on entertainment and conventional western subjects—he is very much aware of that mask.

Priscilla Jane Thompson

Priscilla Jane Thompson trained to be a teacher, but, according to Dabney, ill health kept her from actually becoming one.[54] She never married, living her entire life in Rossmoyne, Ohio, with her sister Clara and brother Garland. She was a long-serving Sunday school teacher at Zion Baptist Church in Cincinnati, reflecting a devotion to Christianity that can be seen in many of her poems.[55] Priscilla died from a stroke in 1942 at the age of 71, after several years of illness.[56]

Priscilla and Aaron seem to have started publishing their poetry and performing publicly around the same time. Aaron published *Morning Songs* in 1899, and Priscilla published *Ethiope Lays* in 1900. The earliest public performances we have found advertised for any of the Thompson siblings are readings by both Aaron and Priscilla at the 1900 Emancipation Day celebration at the Carthage (Ohio) fairgrounds, though it is likely that they had already been performing publicly for some time by then.[57] Despite their parallels early on, however, Priscilla has received more positive attention from scholars than has her brother. Eight of her poems have been anthologized in collections of African-American writing: "The Muse's Favor" (149–151),[58] "Knight of My Maiden Love,"[59] "A Hymn,"[60] "A Prayer" (116),[61] "Freedom at McNealy's" (164–167),[62] "The Husband's Return" (120–123),[63] "A Home Greeting" (128),[64] and "To a Little Colored Boy."[65] One additional poem, "The Snail's Lesson," was anthologized in a collection of poems about nature and Christianity.[66] Facsimile editions of both *Ethiope Lays* and *Gleanings of Quiet Hours* were published in 1988 by The Schomburg Center for Research in Black Culture at the New York Public Library.[67] Even though she wrote on a number of subjects and with quite a bit of linguistic variety, all of the poems scholars have chosen for anthologizing are written in "standard" English (i.e., the non-regional variety of English accepted at the time by publishers and academics as standard for written works). Most of them also refer to racial blackness or slavery, as well. In other words, these anthologies have implicitly defined Priscilla as a poet who wrote about Black subjects in "standard" English. This is strange, given the variety of topics she wrote about and the number of witty dialect poems included in *Gleanings of Quiet Hours*.

Priscilla's poetry has been noted for its focus on Black women, particularly on issues of Black female beauty and subjectivity.[68] Her poems also consistently draw on tropes of nineteenth-century sentimental abolitionist literature and slave narratives. As a result, her two books, *Ethiope Lays* (1900) and *Gleanings of Quiet Hours* (1907), have many direct connections to the literature of the later Harlem Renaissance. Her poetry mixes heroic male figures and strong Black women, with the explicit purpose of uplifting people of color.[69] As she states in her introduction to *Gleanings of Quiet Hours*, "if in any of these humble and simple rhymes, a passage or thought may chance prove a medium through which the race may be elevated ... the writer feels that her efforts is fully repaid" (108). We think that Priscilla is most distinguished from her siblings, and as a poet generally, by her skill at using a variety of poetic personae and linguistic registers to explore intersectional and psychological depth among the Black community, particularly among women.

In 1906, the year of Dunbar's death, the Black-run Indianapolis newspaper *The Recorder* wondered whether Priscilla might be the Black poet to take up his poetic legacy. "Miss Thompson," the writer informs, "is a child of slave parents, who emigrated to Ohio after the late rebellion," and she "evinced a talent for writing poetry, while still a child." The reviewer is supportive of Priscilla's poems, calling them "smooth and original," and noting that they "deal chiefly with the joys and sorrows of her own race." According to the article, Priscilla was also "a talented elocutionist and her recitals [met] with the approval of every audience."[70]

Scholars in the early twentieth century were less appreciative of Priscilla's poetry than scholars in the twenty-first century have been. In 1923 White and Jackson wrote of *Ethiope Lays* that Priscilla "shows greater rhythmic facility and metric variety than her brother, also more narrative" but "her verse is rather ignorant and crude." They describe her as having "rather a sullen, uncomprehending, illiterate hatred." The poems in *Gleanings of Quiet Hours* "show considerable improvement," according to White and Jackson, but "still there are occasional raw crudities and the same fundamental lack of education."[71] White and Jackson are correct that some poems contain grammatical or stylistic problems. Two narrative poems about slavery, "The Fugitive" (111–113) and "The Husband's Return" (120–123), are especially egregious according to mechanical conventions of grammar. The verb tense of each poem slides back and forth between past and present, and there are a few inconsistencies in number between subject and verb. It is possible, however, that these deviations from "standard" English are not errors at all, as we discuss in the "Notes on Editing" (lxix–lxxxi). Both poems focus on a Black man whose masculinity is restored through escape and agency. The escaped slave in "The Fugitive" finds that "his manhood wakes" (lines 5, 54) when he runs from his owner and when he reaches Canada, whereas the escaped slave in "The Husband's Return" is able to overcome the "owner" of his wife and child:

> Young Stephen flung an answer back,
>   With fury in his eye,
> That suddenly did take his breath,
> And paled his face, as if grim death
>   Had dropped down from the sky. (lines 66–70)

The disruption of verb tense in these poems could reflect the psychologically damaging effects of slavery on the characters or the continuing psychological effects of slavery even decades later. Unlike White and Jackson, maybe readers today should be more open to viewing the interpretive possibilities of these "crudities."

Other poems in Priscilla's collection explore the lingering effects of slavery, as well. "Uncle Ike's Holiday" (126–127), in which a Black laborer argues with his white employer over work ethics, shows how the continuing and assumed hierarchical racial order of slavery leads to conflicts in the twentieth century. Uncle Ike is chastised by his employer for celebrating on Emancipation Day. His employer argues,

> "I didn't take you for the man,
>   Kind as I've been to you,
> To leave me in this busy time,
> Tomatoes spoiling on my vines,
>   To loaf a whole day through. (lines 6–10)

Uncle Ike will have none of it and immediately challenges his white employer, explaining that he is celebrating a holiday for Emancipation, which is just as important to him as the Fourth of July is to the employer. It is this shortcoming of whiteness being ignorant of Black American culture, not a Black person's work ethic, Uncle Ike argues, that is at fault for the misunderstanding. Perhaps we can see the same ignorance in White and Jackson's identification of "crudities" in Priscilla's poems.

Despite a few poems that focus on Black masculinity, Priscilla primarily focuses on Black women. "The Muse's Favor" (149–151), for example, explores western conceptions of beauty. Who is celebrated as beautiful? Who is ignored? The poem's speaker writes that the poet has a responsibility and gift to choose their subjects:

> Oh Muse! I crave a favor,
> > Grant but this one unto me;
> Thou hast always been indulgent,
> > So I boldly come to thee.
>
> For oft I list thy singing,
> > And the accents, sweet and clear,
> Like the rhythmic flow of waters,
> > Falls on my ecstatic ear.
>
> But of Caucasia's daughters,
> > So oft I've heard thy lay,
> That the music, too familiar,
> > Falls in sheer monotony. (lines 1–12)

Here, the speaker talks of "Caucasia's daughters" (i.e., white women) and how they have disproportionately been the focus of poetic praise, so often that the "music" of their praise becomes "too familiar, / Falls in sheer monotony" (lines 11–12). The speaker concludes the poem by asking the muse to focus, for once, on Black women:

And now, oh Muse exalted!
   Exchange this old song staid,
For an equally deserving:—
   The oft slighted, Afric maid.

The muse, with smiles, consenting,
   Runs her hand the strings along,
And the harp, as bound by duty,
   Rings out with the tardy song. (lines 13–20)

The muse then sings exactly what the speaker asked for—a poem specifically praising blackness, femininity, and Black women. To drive home the point that this is a celebratory poem, the muse closes each of the six stanzas with a variation of "I sing of thee":

Oh, foully slighted Ethiope maid!
With patience, bearing rude upbraid,
With sweet, refined, retiring grace,
And sunshine lingering in thy face,
With eyes bedewed and pityingly,
I sing of thee, I sing of thee.

Thy dark and misty curly hair,
In small, neat braids entwineth fair,
Like clusters of rich, shining jet,
All wrapt in mist, when sun is set;
Fair maid, I gaze admiringly,
And sing of thee, and sing of thee.

Thy smooth and silky, dusky skin,
Thine eyes of sloe, thy dimple chin,
That pure and simple heart of thine,
'Tis these that make thee half divine;

> Oh maid! I gaze admiringly,
> And sing of thee, and sing of thee. (lines 21–38)

The attention to Black women's physical features—"dark and misty colored hair" and "silky, dusky skin"—both redefines western tropes of beauty and insists that Black women have divine beauty. In other words, while Black bodies were often described as savage, exotic, and animal-like in American literature of the nineteenth and early twentieth centuries, "The Muse's Favor" argues that it is not in spite of their physical features but *because of* them that Black women are "half divine." Prefiguring the "Black Is Beautiful" movement of the 1960s and CaShawn Thompson's viral 2013 hashtag #BlackGirlMagic, "The Muse's Favor" is an early artistic celebration of Black womanhood in spite of, and distinctly separate from, typically white western notions of aesthetic form.

The little domestic vignettes sprinkled throughout *Gleanings of Quiet Hours* add a deeper dimension to Priscilla's representations of Black womanhood. Compare "Just How It Happened" (114–115), for instance, with "The Interrupted Reproof" (163). In "Just How It Happened" a young woman tells her friends how she became engaged. The speaker's middle-class vernacular suggests that the poem is exploring Black middle-class conventions for marriage in the early twentieth century rather than love in general:

> Well, I was at the dresser,
>   A-prinking at my hair,
> When mamma bustled in, and said,
>   "Luvenia, Joe's down-stair."
>
> Of course I was all ready,
>   But say girls, don't you know?
> Just not to seem too anxious,
>   I poked, and came down slow. (lines 1–8)

While the poem deals with a fairly mundane subject, it reveals quite a bit about the socioeconomic status of the speaker: she is educated, has the leisure time to chat with her friends, lives in a house with multiple stories, has time and resources to "prink" at her hair, engages in formal courtship, and has the luxury and presumable economic comfort to strategize about courtship. In contrast, "The Interrupted Reproof" is told from the perspective of a mother who chastises her daughter for playing with dolls rather than focusing on courtship with her beau Eddie:

> Zella Wheeler! did I evah?
>   Playing with yo' ole dolls; Well!
> Great, big gal, here, tall as mammy,
> Big a baby as Estelle!
>   . . .
>
> Yo' ole mammy's not gwine keep it,
>   Ed's gwine 'o hear it sho's you bo'n;
> Shame on you! An' Ed a co'ting.
> Playing dolls heah all the mo'n.
>   . . .
>
> Gwine tell Ed, and gwine tell daddy—
>   What's that noise! Who's that out tha'?
> Give me them dolls, Lawd, here's Eddie!
>   Mussy sakes! Go bresh yo' ha'. (lines 1–24)

Unlike the speaker in "Just How It Happened," Zella is not interested in "prinking" at her hair or getting engaged, even though her mother is clearly anxious to marry her off. The contrast between the mother's insistence on propriety and use of dialect, describing herself as "Yo' ole mammy," reveals a social and domestic situation different from the one in "Just How It Happened." The daughter in "The Interrupted Reproof" does not have the luxury to play, and her personal desires—to defer adulthood and/or marriage to Eddie—are at odds with social expectations and, perhaps, economic reality. The fact that the mother threatens to tell Zella's father and a church elder suggests that the mother, at least, thinks her daughter is flouting social expectations of the community. Both of these poems demonstrate middle-class aspirations in the Black community. "The Interrupted Reproof" reveals conflict between the individual and those community expectations, however.

As in "The Interrupted Reproof," the mothers in poems such as "The Examination" (131–134) and "A Domestic Storm" (178–179) demonstrate the role of Black women in creating and maintaining middle-class expectations in the community. All three poems feature mothers pushing their children to behave in respectable ways. In "The Examination," for example, Lucindy chastises her son Peter for not taking his education seriously and quizzes him on spelling. In "A Domestic Storm" a mother chastises her son Sammy for eating a pie the family received from one of the mother's washing clients: "I'm goin' to whoop you, Sammy Taylor, / Done gone eat nigh half my pie!" (lines 1–2). The poems provide context to explain the passion with which each mother interacts with her children. All three mothers are identified as working-class through occupation and dialect. In "The Examination," for instance, we learn that Lucindy was formerly enslaved; in "A Domestic Storm" the mother notes that the pie was sent from "Miss Julie . . . When Jim cya'ed de washin' home" (lines 25–26), which suggests that the mother helps to support her family by washing. In each poem, the mother is not just annoyed by her child(ren)'s perceived lack of effort but also spurred by circumstances to respond emotionally. In other words, these poems reflect Black women's attempts to "uplift" their children and sympathy toward Black women who might be perceived as overbearing.

Even the poem "Insulted" (173), written from a child's perspective, is ultimately sympathetic to a harsh mother. In this humorous poem a young child who has just been spanked for sticking their finger in a ginger cake and filling the holes with lard complains about how mean their mother is. The indignant child says,

> My Mamma is a mean old sing,
>   An' toss as she tan be;
> I'm doeing to pack my doll trunt,
>   An' doe to G'an'ma Lee. (lines 1–4)

Readers might be amused by the young child's adorable mispronunciation of words or by the child's assumption that the grandmother will be less mean. The last stanza of the poem, however, adds context to explain the mother's anger—context the naïve speaker seems unaware of:

> An' fen she det so lonesome,
>   Like she did las' week, an' kied,
> I won't yun out an' tiss her,
>   I'm doeing 'way, an' hide. (lines 21–24)

For such a short poem, "Insulted" packs a lot of psychological depth. The child does not seem to understand the link between her mother being "lonesome" and being angry with her, but the skillful use of diction and naïve persona allows the reader to see it.

    Priscilla's nuanced use of language and personae in these domestic vignettes is a clear contrast with Aaron's poems, especially in her sympathetic portrayal of Black mothers. Aaron's representation of women was consistently superficial. To be fair, Aaron did redefine western tropes of female beauty in poems such as "Our Girls" (28), "To Helen" (33), and "The Maiden's Song" (70–71), and dialect poems such as "Miss Susie's Social" (46–49), "Reason Why I's Happy" (64), and "Out Among Um" (90–94) express appreciation for young, unmarried Black women. But none of these poems offers any psychological depth or understanding of women. In fact, the speaker of the only poem in Aaron's collection that focuses on a married woman (rather than an unmarried maiden), "After the Honeymoon" (85–87), portrays his wife as a nag and a spendthrift. Priscilla was much more interested in the psychological depth of Black women.

Ann Allen Shockley raises the further possibility of reading Priscilla's poetry through a queer lens, positing, "some might single out two of her romantic poems as woman-identified": "Alberta" and "Evelyn," from Priscilla's first collection, *Ethiope Lays*.[72] Both are love poems to women. To that list, we would add "An Unromantic Awakening," also from *Ethiope Lays*, in which the speaker dreams about kissing a woman: "I drank her warm breath rapt'ously, / As her soft arms my neck entwined" (lines 5–6). Also, "A Home Greeting" (128), in which the speaker describes a "long, ecstatic kiss" with their wife that "drowns all earthly strife" (lines 9–10). And "A Valentine" (138), whose speaker sends a valentine to a girl to "give her a lecture" (line 8). Maybe one could also interpret the reluctance of the young woman in "The Interrupted Reproof" (163) to accept attention from her male suitor as a rejection of heterosexual love. Or read "In the Valley" (181–182) as a conflicted confession to Jesus of same-sex desire:

> My heart craves earthly things;
>   I feel its nature's claim;
> Since Thou didst give me life,
>   Canst I discard an aim?
>
> The hot blood stirs my brain,
>   And sweet dreams to me flock;
> Alas! I see them wrecked
>   Upon Ambition's rock.

> Oh Christ! Come down to earth,
>   An elder brother, be;
> And pilot Thou, my barque,
>   Which drifts capriciously.
>
> Oh wrench me from the toils
>   Of this entangled mesh!
> My spirit strives for Thee,
>   Despite the erring flesh. (lines 13–28)

Priscilla's poetry certainly provides evidence of attraction to women. In fact, most of the love poems in *Gleanings of Quiet Hours* are addressed to women. Does this mean that Priscilla was attracted to women, though? We cannot assume that every poem reflects its author's personal opinions or identities. Priscilla, in fact, adopted a variety of personae in her poems—male and female, adult and child, lower class and middle class—and, as "The Muse's Favor" demonstrates, she was aware of the western convention of love poetry written about white women. The poems that express romantic attraction for women, Black women in particular, could thus reflect a desire for Black women to be seen as the *object* of romantic interest, not necessarily the subject. However, we can, at the very least, argue that a queer reading of her poems is possible.

Clara Ann Thompson

Clara Ann Thompson started publishing later in life than her siblings. She published two collected volumes in her lifetime, *Songs from the Wayside* (1908) and *A Garland of Poems* (1926). She also published two long poems, "What Means This Bleating of the Sheep?" (1921 and 1923) and "There Came Wise Men" (1923) in pamphlet form. These longer poems are included in her later collection, *A Garland of Poems,* and deal explicitly with the morality (or lack thereof) of both white and Black Americans. According to Dabney in *Cincinnati's Colored Citizens,* Clara trained as a teacher, but she taught for only one year before returning to Rossmoyne, where she lived the rest of her life. She was an active member of the Baptist church, the NAACP, and the YWCA, and was considered a "fine elocutionist."[73] She died in 1949 at the age of 80, the last of the eleven Thompson siblings.

Clara wrote in the foreword to *A Garland of Poems* that she had never intended to be a poet, but was rather interested in writing novels. "Thoughts that I have intended to express in long chapters of prose," she wrote, "I have expressed in just a few verses of poetry."[74] Maybe it was better that she wrote poetry after all, because of the three Thompson poets, Clara has received the most scholarly attention. Ten of her poems, all from *Songs from the Wayside,* have been anthologized by scholars in collections of African-American literature: "His Answer" (207),[75] "Mrs. Johnson Objects" (212–213),[76] "Uncle Rube on the Race Problem" (224–228),[77] "I'll Follow Thee" (220),[78] "Out of the Deep" (234),[79] "The Angel's Message" (excerpt, 250–252),[80] "Storm-Beaten" (253),[81] "Johnny's Pet Superstition" (203–205),[82] "The Easter Bonnet" (262–263),[83] and "A Lullaby" (245).[84] While this mix of poems is generally representative of Clara's writing—especially the emphasis on religion and the direct attention to issues of race—it does overrepresent dialect. Of the 36 poems in *Songs from the Wayside,* only eight are written in dialect. Almost all of those dialect poems have been anthologized, which gives the false impression that Clara wrote primarily in dialect.

A facsimile edition of *Songs from the Wayside* was published in 1988 by The Schomburg Center for Research in Black Culture at the New York Public Library alongside Priscilla's collections.[85] In 1996 *A Garland of Poems* was published in a volume with J. Pauline Smith's *"Exceeding Riches" and Other Verse* and Mazie

Earhart Clark's *Garden of Memories*.[86] Most recently, Nikki Grimes included two of Clara's poems—"Life and Death" and "The Minor Key," both from *A Garland of Poems*—in her 2017 children's book *One Last Word: Wisdom from the Harlem Renaissance*. Grimes uses these poems as a starting point to write new poems by the "golden shovel" method.[87] Clara's later collection, *A Garland of Poems,* put her in closer proximity to the writers of the Harlem Renaissance, which might help to explain why she has had slightly more scholarly recognition than her siblings.

Compared to the poetry of her siblings, Clara's is the most direct, the most engaged in politics, and the most polished. Critics have noted the didactic and moralizing tone of some of her poems, which are a bit old-fashioned for the tastes of later twentieth-century critics and scholars. Joan Sherman, for example, argues in *Collected Black Women's Poetry*, "The Thompson sisters' output [was] … noteworthy only in its quantity."[88] White and Jackson, the same scholars who wrote that Aaron's "grammar is somewhat faulty" and "his diction is poor" and that Priscilla's "verse is rather ignorant and crude," wrote that the poems in Clara's *Songs from the Wayside* are "of better quality than those of her brother and sister." "She has more restraint," they continue. "The religious note seems a bit more impressive throughout than that of her brother and sister … and the artistic finish is better. There are not so many crudities of rhyme, diction, and grammar." Despite this relatively positive assessment, however, White and Jackson conclude that Clara "has no breadth of view, or intensity or much imagination, and not much culture."[89]

Besides the fact that Clara's poems tend to be more polished than those of her siblings, White and Jackson also seem to prefer the approach to issues of race in some of her poems. Of all the poems written by the Thompson siblings, White and Jackson chose to anthologize Clara's "His Answer" (207) and "Mrs. Johnson Objects" (212–213). "His Answer" is a religious poem that advises patience for one's current sorrows, whereas in "Mrs. Johnson Objects" a Black mother scolds her son for wanting to play with "po' white trash" who are "spilte" (lines 5, 20). Both poems argue that one should be content with one's lot in life, which is in line with Booker T. Washington's approach to the so-called race issue. While White and Jackson identify Priscilla's approach to race as a "sullen, uncomprehending, illiterate hatred," they argue that Clara's "race feeling is not bitter and not without recognition of the Negro's obligations and deficiencies."[90] Their critical assessment of the Thompsons, therefore, seems to be influenced by their own beliefs about the "race problem" of the early twentieth century. On the whole, however, Clara's poems do not subscribe to Washington's approach.

In the foreword to *A Garland of Poems,* Clara argues that her "restraint" in representing race issues was an intentional choice. She writes,

> I have endeavored to be sincere and fair in all the subjects treated, especially in those pertaining to my people, whom I love very dearly. So in this book and also in my first book, "Songs from the Wayside," I have endeavored to present both sides of the subject, knowing that no problem can be truly solved in any other way.[91]

And, in fact, this intentional attempt to present balance can be seen within many of Clara's poems in *Songs from the Wayside.* "The Old and the New" (254–259) offers the opinions of both the younger generation and the older generations on "shouting" in church; "Johnny's Pet Superstition" (203–204) juxtaposes southern rural superstition and northern book learning. What is significant in this approach is Clara's acknowledgement that she is entering volatile debates on race: Aaron advertised himself as an entertainer, Priscilla wrote for racial uplift, but Clara used poetry for political and social problem-solving.

Clara's efforts "to be sincere and fair" and to "present both sides of the subject" do not mean, however, that she does not express strong opinions. Despite a few poems like "His Answer" (207) that advise patience, some of Clara's poems echo DuBois's call for faster progress. In fact, the recurring character Uncle Rube is a fictional persona that challenges many ideas of white Americans. "Uncle Rube on the Race Problem" (224–228), for example, gives Uncle Rube's answers to a white audience's questions about race relations in the United States. The first two lines of the poem establish an antagonistic relationship from the start: "How'd I solve 'de Negro Problum'?" Uncle Rube asks. "Gentlemen, don't like dat wo'd!" (lines 1–2). According to Uncle Rube the phrase "Negro Problem" automatically assumes that Black people are the problem, when, in his view, white people are the real problem in issues such as "amalmagation" (i.e., miscegenation) and Jim Crow laws. By expressing fears about the mixing of people of different racial identities, he argues, white people are really just trying to disenfranchise Black people, "Dat dis 'malgamation fright's / Jes' got up by you smawt white-folks, / Keep fum givin' us ou' rights" (lines 110–112). He has similar thoughts about Jim Crow laws and segregation:

> "Be a nation in a nation"?
>   Now you're talkin' like a fool!
> Whut you mean by "'Plur'bus unyun—"?
>   Many nations 'neath one rule.
>
> Not go'n' back on dat ol' motto,
>   Dat has made yo' country's name,
> Jest because de race you brung here
>   Ax you fah a little claim? (lines 117–124)

In "Uncle Rube's Defense" (200), he argues that white people have a double standard when it comes to poor behavior:

> White-folks a-thievin' and rahin' an' kickin',
>   Uddah white-folks ez still ez a mouse;
> Aftahwhile, somebody steals a few chickens,
>   Den, dey wan' to search old Deacon Jones' house.
> ...
> Ev'ry low trick dat de black man's a-doin'
>   'Flects right back on de race, as a whole;
> But de low co'se dat de white man's pursuin'
>   Casts not a blot on his good brudder's soul. (lines 5–16)

White people, Uncle Rube argues, are happy to assign blame of one person to the entire Black race, but do not do the same for themselves.

Uncle Rube's responses to the presumed objections of his white audience might suggest the reason Clara chose to voice these criticisms through a fictional persona. In "Uncle Rube on the Race Problem," Uncle Rube acknowledges that his white audience will be put off by his honest opinions, asking,

> Whut you say? I'm too hawd on you?
>   Whut you 'spected me to do,
> When you axed me my opinion?
>   Tell you somepin' wusn't true? (lines 41–44)

Readers will recognize that even though he does not speak in a genteel, educated dialect, "Uncle Rube" is no rube at all. In fact, Uncle Rube is very informed on political and intellectual debates of the time. He is also very critical of white people's role in the so-called race problem.

Even the title of the collection, *Songs from the Wayside,* is a subtle indictment of white culture. It plays on the title of Henry Wadsworth Longfellow's famous 1863 poem *Tales of a Wayside Inn,* which many have read as a comment on American national identity. In Longfellow's long narrative poem, seven characters—the aristocratic landlord of British descent, the student of western classics, the Spanish Jewish trader of fine goods, the fiery Sicilian, the Norwegian musician, the Christian theologian, and the poet—gather around a pub fireplace to enjoy each other's company and tell stories. The landlord's tale, for instance, is the story of Paul Revere's ride. In essence, each character explains through their story how their national/ethnic culture contributes to the melting pot of American culture. As the title of Clara's collection points out, however, Black Americans are not included in this convivial gathering at the hearth of American culture. In other words, Black Americans are not invited into the Wayside Inn but rather left at the wayside.

Clara's directness is apparent throughout *Songs from the Wayside,* not just in the poems that address race issues. Personal regret and disillusionment permeate the entire collection, even the love poems. The speaker of "The After-Glow of Pain" (209–210), for instance, argues that personal disappointments may be painful for a while, but ultimately they result in fine sentiments. The male speaker of "Parted" (214–215) learns that even though his beloved has forgiven him for an indiscretion she will never again love him in the same way. And "Hope Deferred" (229) is a depressing lyric on the failure of hope:

> Hope strives in vain to cheer the way,
> With promise of a coming day,
>   When life will be more sweet.
> I cannot listen to her song,
> The night is dark, the way is long.
>   A bitterness comes o'er my soul,
> I cry, beneath the gloom,
>   Oh Hope, thou seemest but a myth,
> To lure us to our doom! (lines 17–25)

Though the reader might expect or hope for a turn in the speaker's mindset in this poem, it never comes. Even the speaker of the obligatory Christmas poem in the collection, "The Christmas Rush" (217–218), manages to side-step the Christmas spirit by complaining about how annoying Christmas shopping is:

> The streets were crowded with people,
>   And at last when we reached the stores,
> There was such a mass of shoppers,
>   We could scarcely pass through the doors.
>
> We forced our way to the counter,
>   This bitter truth to learn—
> That others were there before us,
>   So we must await our turn.
>
> At last it came, and we purchased,
>   And then—'twas enough to derange!
> We had the self-same experience,
>   Awaiting our parcels and change. (lines 13–24)

And then there are the poems that refer to a woman who regrets rejecting a proposal from her suitor: "If Thou Shouldst Return" (211), "She Sent Him Away" (233), and "Oh List to My Song!" (260).

Many poems in *Songs from the Wayside* identify Christianity as the solution to this malaise. In "Doubt" (208), for instance, the light that shines "through darkness and dread" is "a Savior's guiding love" (lines 11, 14). "The Easter Light" (221–223) describes a grieving woman who finds comfort in church on Easter Sunday while listening to a solo singer in the choir: "The maiden listens— ah! the hot tears start, / And melt the ice that o'er her heart has grown" (lines 47–48). Perhaps the most plaintive expression of faith is "Out of the Deep" (234), in which the speaker cries,

> I cannot, cannot cease to cry to Thee,
>   For oh, my God, this heart is not my own,
>   And as the streams press ever to the sea,
>   My heart turns to Thy throne. (lines 13–16)

Similarly, in "Storm-Beaten" (253), the speaker pleads,

> Weary, worn, and sorrow-laden,
>   Jesus, I have come to Thee;
>   Shield me from the darts of Satan;
>   Set my fettered spirit free. (lines 1–4)

While these religious poems do not all address race specifically, they are nevertheless thematically reminiscent of Dunbar's "We Wear the Mask." In fact, *Songs from the Wayside* as a whole echoes Dunbar's poem. The speaker of "We Wear the Mask" argues, "We smile, but, O great Christ, our cries / To thee from tortured souls arise" (lines 10–11), whereas the speaker of Clara's poem "Out of the Deep" laments, "I cannot, cannot cease to cry to Thee, / For oh, my God, this heart is not my own" (lines 13–14). Clara's *Songs from the Wayside* uses "balance" as a mask but nevertheless reveals what lies beneath it. In the character of Uncle Rube and other poetic personae, Clara used the mask trope to express critiques while distancing herself from them. But many poems, such as "Out of the Deep" and "Storm-Beaten," seem to express her own resonance with Dunbar's poem.

Clara's 1926 collection *A Garland of Poems* offers a distinct contrast to *Songs from the Wayside*. If Clara was wearing a mask in *Songs of the Wayside,* she was wearing sparring gloves in *A Garland of Poems.* While this later collection includes some generic poems about love and nature, it is firmly embedded in its post-WWI moment. Many poems are dedicated to specific events: Christmas 1916, the death of Booker T. Washington, the departure of Black troops from Cincinnati to Fort Sherman in WWI, the return of Black troops from fighting in WWI, Easter 1919, the 91st anniversary of Union Baptist Church in Cincinnati, and so on. Some poems also have an extremely didactic tone. "You'll Have to Come Back to the Road," "To Obey Is Better Than Sacrifice," "Be True to the Best," "Let Us Get Back to God," "What Means This Bleating of the Sheep?" and "Our Side of the Race Problem" all offer direct address on appropriate behavior.

The poems in *A Garland of Poems* may, as Clara wrote in the foreword, show both sides of the so-called race problem, but only because Clara took everyone to task. Uncle Rube appears again in a few poems, such as "Uncle Rube on Church Quarrels," but Clara's criticisms were not voiced just by her fictional persona in her later collection. For example, in "What Means This Bleating of the Sheep?" the unidentified speaker writes explicitly on the Civil War, emancipation, and the failings of the U.S. republic:

> America, proud freedom's land,
>   Thy flag is trailing in the dust!
> Where are thy boasted precepts grand,
>   Your pledge of faith: "In God We Trust?"
> ...
>
> Alas! they did not loose his bands
>   Because they hated slavery,
> But that their fair united land,
>   Might ever undivided be.[92]

This long poem argues that the Civil War was not really about slavery and that the United States was failing to fulfill its moral promises. Chastising both the bigotry of the Klan and the political outlooks of new immigrants to the United States, the speaker provides the reader with an outlook that is both racialized "other" in America and empowered enough to say,

> E'en now your wards of foreign lands,
>   Are forging chains of Anarchy;
>   And while you chain the African,
>   They'll bind you in their slavery.[93]

The Black-run Cincinnati newspaper *The Union* reported that Black audiences were receptive to Clara's poem, noting, "Miss Clara Thompson of Rossmoyne, O. is receiving much applause reciting her splendid poem: 'What Means This Bleating of the Sheep' in Indianapolis, Ind."[94]

Similarly, "Our Side of the Race Problem" chastises the Black community:

> I come to you, my countrymen,
> Come with and [sic] earnest plea,
> I pray the God of Israel,
> That you'll lend ear to me.
> For, like those murm'ring men of old,
> You wander in distress;
> You've left Egyptian slavery,
> To find the wilderness.
>
> …
>
> I speak not of the barriers,
> Your proud white brothers place,
> I'm speaking of the deadly foes,
> That rise in your own race.[95]

As the poems in *A Garland of Poems* suggest, by the 1920s Clara was not interested in wearing any masks. *Songs from the Wayside,* however, is a clear-eyed explication of the mask in the first decade of the twentieth century.

The Thompsons in the Twenty-First Century

Aaron Belford Thompson, Priscilla Jane Thompson, and Clara Ann Thompson wrote, performed, and published poetry during a transitional period in American history. The years between Reconstruction and WWI were punctuated by regular violence against Black Americans as the United States struggled to be a multi-ethnic and multi-racial democratic nation. The Thompson poets were consciously writing within and about that cultural moment. And yet their poems still resonate more than 100 years later. Discussions about racism continue, as evidenced by the Black Lives Matter movement, *The New York Times*'s 1619 Project (which reframes American history through the lens of slavery and the contributions of Black Americans), and mainstream debates about "Critical Race Theory." In some ways, the Thompsons' poetry has as much to say about early twenty-first-century America as it did about early twentieth-century America. Contemporary readers will be able to see in the poetry of the Thompson siblings the continued tension of American plurality.

Acknowledgments

We would like to thank the many people who helped us with our reasearch into the Thompson siblings for this introduction. The global COVID-19 pandemic prevented us from traveling to conduct research, but the following people were willing to help remotely, via email, phone, and online interviews: Stephen Headley at the Cincinnati Public Library; Valerie Daniels and Paul George at the Hamilton County (Ohio) Recorder's Office; Melissa Pearse at the Hamilton County (Ohio) Probate Court; Tutti Jackson at the Ohio History Connection; and author Lester Horwitz. Thank you for sharing your time and expertise with us. Patricia Oman's research was supported by a short sabbatical leave from Hastings College in the 2020–2021 academic year.

We would also like to acknowledge the Indianapolis and Cincinnati community members and historians who keep local history in those cities alive and accessible. Online blogs such as *Invisible Indianapolis* and *Queens of Queen City* provide important links between the past and the present. Please check out their excellent blog posts on the Thompson siblings.

Notes

1. Among published accounts of the Thompson family, dates of birth are somewhat uncertain, especially for Clara. Joan Sherman in *Invisible Poets: Afro-Americans of the Nineteenth Century* (University of Illinois Press, 1974) places Clara's birth in 1887, which would make her the youngest of the siblings. That would also place her birth *after* the death of her parents. (See note 4.) Ann Allen Shockley in *Afro-American Women Writers, 1746–1933: An Anthology and Critical Guide* (G.K. Hall, 1988) and Mary Anne Stewart Boelcskevy in *Clara Ann Thompson, J. Pauline Smith, Mazie Earhart Clark: Voices in the Poetic Tradition* (G.K. Hall, 1996) both place Clara's birth date at 1869. Census and other civil records provide somewhat more definitive dates of birth and death. The 1900 federal census lists Clara's birth date as January 1869, Priscilla's birth date as February 1871, and Aaron's birth date as April 1873. In an affidavit dated September 19, 1946, Clara identified her own birth month/year as January 1870. Priscilla and Aaron's birth and death years are verified on the tombstone they share with brothers Edward and Garland in United American Cemetery in East Madisonville, Ohio. Death certificates for the poets are less helpful in determining birth dates. While they verify the dates of death, they do not have reliable information on birth dates. Priscilla's death certificate does not include a birth date/year (and her brother Garland is listed as her father, as reported by Clara). Aaron's death certificate lists his birth date as April 1883, seven years after his mother's death. This information was reported by his second wife, Hallie. Because it does not match any other records and because Hallie did not know the name and birthplace of Aaron's mother,

we assume that the birth year listed on his death certificate is incorrect. Clara's death date is confirmed by newspaper obituaries. 1900 United States census, Hamilton County, Ohio, population schedule, Sycamore Township, p. 7 (penned), p. 227 (stamped), enumeration district 288, dwelling 126, family 128, "Clara Thompson," "Priscilla Thompson," "Aaron Thompson," FHL microfilm 1241282, digital image, *Ancestry. com;* Hamilton County, Ohio, affidavit for transfer and record of real estate inherited, deed book 2196, pp. 386–388, Clara Ann Thompson, 19 September 1946, digital image, Recorder's Office, Hamilton County; Samuel Thompson, Garland Thompson, Aaron Thompson, Priscilla Thompson, grave marker, United American Cemetery, East Madisonville, Hamilton County, Ohio, digital image, *FindAGrave.com;* Aaron Belford Thompson, death certificate, 26 January 1929, registered no. 2453, Indiana State Board of Health, digital image, *Ancestry.com;* Pricilla [sic] Thompson, death certificate, 4 May 1942, no. [illegible], State of Ohio, Bureau of Vital Statistics, digital image, *FamilySearch. org;* Clara Ann Thompson, obituary, *The Cincinnati Enquirer,* 20 March 1949, p. 30, digital image, *newspapers.com.*

2. We have been unable to locate a copy of this pamphlet, though Aaron published one of the poems, "Chick-O-Ma Craney Crow," in *The Recorder* (Indianapolis, Indiana), 12 February 1927, p. 5; "Thompson (Aaron Belford). Indianapolis. Rhymes of Childhood," *Catalogue of Copyright Entries, Part 1: Books, Group 2,* vol. 21, part 1 (Library of Congress, 1925), p. 2117, *books.google.com.*

3. John Henry and Clara Jane's birthplace (Virginia) is noted on many documents, including federal censuses and death certificates for many of their children. We do not know where in Virginia they were born, however. 1870 United States census, Hamilton County, Ohio, population schedule, West ⅔ Sycamore Township, Reading Post Office, p. 24 (penned), dwelling 163, family 160, "John Thompson," "Clara Thompson," NARA roll M593_1208, p. 673B, digital image, *Ancestry. com;* 1880 United States census, Hamilton County, Ohio, population schedule, Sycamore Township, p. 24 (penned), enumeration district 104, dwelling 213, family 223, "J.H. Thompson," NARA roll 1023, p.

510D, digital image, *Ancestry.com;* 1900 United States census, Hamilton County, Ohio, population schedule, Sycamore Township, p. 7 (penned), p. 227 (stamped), enumeration district 288, dwelling 126, family 128, "Garland Thompson," "Clara Thompson," "Priscilla Thompson," "Aaron Thompson," FHL microfilm 1241282, digital image, *Ancestry.com;* 1910 United States census, Hamilton County, Ohio, population schedule, Sycamore Township, p. 4A (penned), p. 167 (stamped), enumeration district 358, dwelling 68, family 72, "Garland Y. Thompson," "Clara A. Thompson," "Priscilla J. Thompson," NARA roll T624_1196, p. 4A, digital image, *Ancestry.com;* 1920 United States census, Hamilton County, Ohio, population schedule, Sycamore Township, p. 11A (penned), p. 204 (stamped), enumeration district 520, dwelling 218, family 218, "Garland Thompson," "Clara Thompson," "Percilla [sic] Thompson," NARA roll T625_1396, p. 11A, digital image, *Ancestry.com;* 1910 United States census, Marion County, Indiana, population schedule, Wayne Township, Indianapolis, p. 8A (penned), p. 270 (stamped), enumeration district 250, dwelling 166, family 169, "Aaron B. Thompson," NARA roll T624_367, p. 8A, digital image, *Ancestry.com;* 1920 United States census, Marion County, Indiana, population schedule, Wayne Township, Indianapolis, p. 6B (penned), enumeration district 251, dwelling 133, family 145, "Aaron Thompson," NARA roll T625_455, p. 6B, digital image, *Ancestry.com;* Aaron Belford Thompson, death certificate; Edward Thompson, death certificate, 8 March 1917, File No. 18356, State of Ohio, Bureau of Vital Statistics, digital image, *FamilySearch.org;* Samuel Thompson, death certificate, 17 October 1909, File No. 51493, State of Ohio, Bureau of Vital Statistics, digital image, *FamilySearch.org;* Garland Y. Thompson, death certificate, 13 June 1938, File No. 34830, State of Ohio, Bureau of Vital Statistics, digital image, *FamilySearch.org.*

4. The names and death dates of John Henry and Clara Jane Thompson and all their children are confirmed by Clara in an affidavit dated September 19, 1946. To sell the family farm, Clara had to document names, addresses, and/or death dates for her parents and all their descendants. This document does not mention Charles Thompson,

who is listed with the family and reported to be 15 years old in the 1870 federal census. This census record is the only record we found for him (though there are several Charles Thompsons recorded in Ohio during the Thompson siblings' lifetimes). He may have been a cousin or uncle to the Thompson siblings, or he may be one of the unnamed siblings in the document who died in "infancy" (Clara's infancy, that is). Affidavit for transfer and record of real estate inherited, deed book 2196, pp. 386–388, Clara Ann Thompson, 19 September 1946; 1870 United States census, Hamilton County, Ohio, population schedule, West ⅔ Sycamore Township, Reading Post Office, p. 24 (penned), dwelling 163, family 160, "Charles Thompson," NARA roll M593_1208, p. 673B, digital image, *Ancestry.com*.

5. We do not know how the Thompsons relocated from Virginia to Kentucky, but most census, death, and military records name Kentucky as the birthplace of the four oldest children: Samuel, Edward, Beverly, and Garland. (We found two conflicting records that list Garland's birthplace as Ohio: the 1920 U.S. census and Garland's death certificate, information on which was reported by Priscilla.) 1870 United States census, Hamilton County, Ohio, population schedule, West ⅔ Sycamore Township, Reading Post Office, p. 24 (penned), dwelling 163, family 160, "Samuel Thompson," "Edward Thompson," "Beverly Thompson," "Garling [sic] Thompson," NARA roll M593_1208, p. 673B, digital image, *Ancestry.com;* 1880 United States census, Hamilton County, Ohio, population schedule, Sycamore Township, p. 24 (penned), enumeration district 104, dwelling 213, family 223, "Garling [sic] Thompson," NARA roll 1023, p. 510D, digital image, *Ancestry. com;* Samuel Thompson, death certificate; 1880 United States census, Hamilton County, Ohio, population schedule, Columbia Township, p. 7 (penned), p. 88 (stamped), enumeration district 85, dwelling 63, family 63, "Ed. Thompson," NARA roll 1022, p. 88C, digital image, *Ancestry.com;* 1900 United States census, Hamilton County, Ohio, population schedule, Columbia Township, p. 3 (penned), p. 191 (stamped), enumeration district 286, dwelling 50, family 55, "Edward Thompson," FHL microfilm 1241282, digital image, *Ancestry.com;* 1910

United States census, Hamilton County, Ohio, population schedule, Columbia Township, p. 11A (penned), p. 232 (stamped), enumeration district 310, dwelling 217, family 227, "Edward F. Thompson," NARA roll T624_1195, p. 11A, digital image, *Ancestry.com;* Edward Thompson, death certificate; 1900 United States census, Hamilton County, Ohio, population schedule, Sycamore Township, p. 7 (penned), p. 227 (stamped), enumeration district 288, dwelling 126, family 128, "Garland Thompson," FHL microfilm 1241282, digital image, *Ancestry.com;* 1910 United States census, Hamilton County, Ohio, population schedule, Sycamore Township, p. 4A (penned), p. 167 (stamped), enumeration district 358, dwelling 68, family 72, "Garland Y. Thompson," NARA roll T624_1196, p. 4A, digital image, *Ancestry.com;* 1920 United States census, Hamilton County, Ohio, population schedule, Sycamore Township, p. 11A (penned), p. 204 (stamped), enumeration district 520, dwelling 218, family 218, "Garland Thompson," NARA roll T625_1396, p. 11A, digital image, *Ancestry.com;* Garland Y. Thompson, death certificate.

6. 1870 United States census, Hamilton County, Ohio, population schedule, West ⅔ Sycamore Township, Reading Post Office, p. 24 (penned), dwelling 163, family 160, "Garling [sic] Thompson," NARA roll M593_1208, p. 673B, digital image, *Ancestry.com;* 1880 United States census, Hamilton County, Ohio, population schedule, Sycamore Township, p. 24 (penned), enumeration district 104, dwelling 213, family 223, "Garling [sic] Thompson," NARA roll 1023, p. 510D, digital image, *Ancestry.com;* Wendell P. Dabney, *Cincinnati's Colored Citizens* (The Dabney Publishing Company, 1926), pp. 316, 318–320.

7. Lester V. Horwitz, *The Longest Raid of the Civil War: Little-Known & Untold Stories of Morgan's Raid into Kentucky, Indiana & Ohio* (Farmcourt Publishing, 1999), p. 125.

8. "Deer Park: A Courageous Bluff," John Hunt Morgan Heritage Trail, https://www.ohiohistory.org/OHC/media/OHC-Media/Documents/morgans_raid_trail_signs.pdf

9. 1870 United States census, Hamilton County, Ohio, population schedule, West ⅔ Sycamore Township, Reading Post Office, p. 24

(penned), dwelling 163, family 160, "John Thompson," "Clara Thompson," NARA roll M593_1208, p. 673B, digital image, *Ancestry. com;* 1870 United States census, Hamilton County, Ohio, population schedule, West ⅔ Sycamore Township, Reading Post Office, p. 23 (penned), dwelling 162, family 159, "John Schenck," "Amelia Schenck," NARA roll M593_1208, p. 673A, digital image, *Ancestry.com.*

10. 1910 United States census, Hamilton County, Ohio, population schedule, Sycamore Township, p. 4A (penned), p. 167 (stamped), enumeration district 358, dwelling 68, family 72, "Garland Y. Thompson," "Clara A. Thompson," "Priscilla J. Thompson," NARA roll T624_1196, p. 4A, digital image, *Ancestry.com;* 1910 United States census, Hamilton County, Ohio, population schedule, Sycamore Township, p. 4A (penned), p. 167 (stamped), enumeration district 358, dwelling 76, family 81, "Ida R. Schenck," NARA roll T624_1196, p. 4A, digital image, *Ancestry.com.*

11. 1870 United States census, Hamilton County, Ohio, population schedule, West ⅔ Sycamore Township, Reading Post Office, p. 24 (penned), dwelling 163, family 160, "Garling [sic] Thompson," "Emma Thompson," NARA roll M593_1208, p. 673B, digital image, *Ancestry. com.*

12. See note 6.

13. Dabney, *Cincinnati's Colored Citizens,* 316.

14. 1870 United States census, Hamilton County, Ohio, population schedule, West ⅔ Sycamore Township, Reading Post Office, p. 24 (penned), dwelling 163, family 160, "John Thompson," "Clara Thompson," NARA roll M593_1208, p. 673B, digital image, *Ancestry. com;* 1880 United States census, Hamilton County, Ohio, population schedule, Sycamore Township, p. 24 (penned), enumeration district 104, dwelling 213, family 223, "J.H. Thompson," NARA roll 1023, p. 510D, digital image, *Ancestry.com.*

15. Hamilton County, Ohio, deed book 456, pp. 301–303, Elsey E. Nelson and James Nelson & John Henry Thompson, 29 April 1876, digital image, Recorder's Office, Hamilton County; Hamilton County, Ohio, deed book 456, pp. 303–304, Calvin N. Deem and Marilda

C. Deem & J.H. and Clara Thompson, 29 April 1876, digital image, Recorder's Office, Hamilton County; Hamilton County, Ohio, deed book 456, pp. 304–305, Thomas A. Stevens & John Henry Thompson and Clara Thompson, 29 April 1876, digital image, Recorder's Office, Hamilton County; "Real estate transfers," *Cincinnati Daily Gazette,* 1 May 1876, p. 3.

16. The first poem in Clara's book *Songs from the Wayside* is titled "To My Dead Brother" (199) and probably refers to Beverly, who died in 1879, at the age of 17. Affidavit for transfer and record of real estate inherited, deed book 2196, pp. 386–388, Clara Ann Thompson, 19 September 1946.

17. In the poem "To a Deceased Friend" (143–144) Priscilla writes of a family friend, Mrs. Polly Dixon, who acted as a foster mother to the children after their mother died. The only record we have been able to find for Polly Dixon is in a list of letters waiting at a post office. "Advertised letters," *Cincinnati Daily Commercial,* 8 November 1862, p. 4.

18. 1900 United States census, Hamilton County, Ohio, population schedule, Sycamore Township, p. 7 (penned), p. 227 (stamped), enumeration district 288, dwelling 126, family 128, "Garland Thompson," FHL microfilm 1241282, digital image, *Ancestry.com;* Hamilton County, Ohio, deed book 2207, pp. 264–265, Clara Ann Thompson & Carl A. Widman and August Hoffman, 13 November 1946, digital image, Recorder's Office, Hamilton County; affidavit for transfer and record of real estate inherited, deed book 2196, pp. 386–388, Clara Ann Thompson, 19 September 1946.

19. In 1908, Aaron and his wife lived at 2123 Howard St. (R.L. Polk & Co.'s Indianapolis City Directory [R.L Polk & Co., 1908], p. 1282, *Ancestry.com*), but their address in the 1909 city directory is 2109 Howard St. (R.L. Polk & Co.'s Indianapolis City Directory [R.L. Polk & Co., 1909], p. 1297, *Ancestry.com*). See also 1910 United States census, Marion County, Indiana, population schedule, Wayne Township, Indianapolis, p. 8A (penned), p. 270 (stamped), enumeration district 250, dwelling 166, family 169, "Aaron B. Thompson," NARA

roll T624_367, p. 8A, digital image, *Ancestry.com*; 1920 United States census, Marion County, Indiana, population schedule, Wayne Township, Indianapolis, p. 6B (penned), enumeration district 251, dwelling 133, family 145, "Aaron Thompson," NARA roll T625_455, p. 6B, digital image, *Ancestry.com*.

20. "Aaron Belford Thompson, Indiana's colored poet author of three successful and popular books," *The Recorder* (Indianapolis, Indiana), 23 March 1912, p. 1. We assume the "valuable Real Estate near Cincinnati" is the family farm, which Aaron co-owned with his siblings.

21. Hamilton County, Ohio, deed book 1429, p. 633, Ralph H. Inott & Garland Y. Thompson, 18 October 1927, digital image, Recorder's Office, Hamilton County; Hamilton County, Ohio, volume XX, pp. 478–480, estate 137558, the last will and testament of Garland Y. Thompson, 21 September 1945, Probate Court, Hamilton County; Hamilton County, Ohio, volume unknown, pp. 480–482, estate 149146, the last will and testament of Priscilla Jane Thompson, 21 September 1945, Probate Court, Hamilton County; Hamilton County, Ohio, volume 296, pp. 467–468, estate 173881, the last will and testament of Clara A. Thompson, 23 March 1949, Probate Court, Hamilton County; Hamilton County, Ohio, deed book 2378, pp. 51–52, Clara Ann Thompson & Emma Smith, 21 September 1949, digital image, Recorder's Office, Hamilton County; "Book of life is concluded for Clara Thompson, poet," *Cincinnati Enquirer*, 20 March 1949.

22. Aaron Belford Thompson, *Echoes of Spring* (self-published, 1901), p. v.

23. Priscilla Jane Thompson, *Ethiope Lays* (self-published, 1899), p. ix.

24. Clara Ann Thompson, *A Garland of Poems* (The Christopher Publishing House, 1926), p. 5.

25. Dabney, *Cincinnati's Colored Citizens*, p. 316. Cincinnati newspapers recorded some of the awards Garland won for wood carving, including second place in the "Specimen wood carving by amateur" category of the 1893 Carthage Fair, held by the Hamilton County Agricultural Society. "A Brilliant Close of the Carthage Fair," *Cincinnati*

Commercial Gazette, 19 August 1893, p. 5; "End of the Fair," *The Cincinnati Tribune,* 19 August 1893, p. 3.

26. "Lynchings of 1906," *The Colored American Magazine,* vol. 12, issue 3 (March 1907), p. 225, *Archive.org.*

27. Joan R. Sherman, ed., *African-American Poetry of the Nineteenth Century: An Anthology* (University of Illinois Press, 1992), p. 8.

28. Paul Laurence Dunbar, "We Wear the Mask," *Lyrics of Lowly Life* (Dodd, Mead and Company, 1898), p. 167.

29. Booker T. Washington, ed., *The Negro Problem: A Series of Articles by Representative American Negroes of To-Day* (James Pott & Company, 1903).

30. See issues 1 (June 1904) to 12 (December 1904) of Volume 7 of *The Colored American Magazine.*

31. "June Weddings," *The Recorder* (Indianapolis, Indiana), 14 June 1902, p. 4; "Marriages: Aaron B. Thompson and Luella Dudley," *The Indianapolis Sun,* 20 June 1902, p. 7; "Marriage Licenses," *The Indianapolis Journal,* 20 June 1902, p. 14; Luella Thompson, death certificate, 5 March 1922, registered no. 9266, Indiana State Board of Health, digital image, *Ancestry.com;* Aaron Belford Thompson, death certificate.

32. Indiana, U.S., Marriage Index, 1800–1941, "Aaron B. Thompson," 16 October 1922, *Ancestry.com*; "Marriage licenses," *The Indianapolis Star,* 17 October 1922, p. 17.

33. Sherman, *Invisible Poets,* p. 208.

34. Aaron Belford Thompson, death certificate. Heart problems seem to have run in the family. Garland's death certificate lists "chronic myocarditis" as his cause of death. Garland Y. Thompson, death certificate. Samuel's death certificate lists "mitral regurgitation" and "valvular heart disease" as his cause of death. Samuel Thompson, death certificate. "Herpaticus in heart" is listed on Priscilla's death certificate as a contributing factor in her death from cerebral hemorrhage. Pricilla [sic] Thompson, death certificate.

35. Dabney, *Cincinnati's Colored Citizens,* p. 318.

36. "Riley Praises Young Negro Poet," *The Indianapolis Star,* 28 July 1907, p. 1.

37. "Mr. Aaron Belford Thompson, Indiana's Colored Poet Author of Three Successful and Popular Books," *The Recorder* (Indianapolis, Indiana), 23 March 1912, p. 1.

38. See note 2. The title of this pamphlet seems to pay homage to an 1890 book of the same name by James Whitcomb Riley.

39. Newman Ivey White and Walter Clinton Jackson, *An Anthology of Verse by American Negroes* (Trinity College Press, 1924), pp. 232–233.

40. Sherman, *Invisible Poets*, p. 208.

41. "Another Negro Poet," *The Commercial Tribune* (Cincinnati, Ohio), 10 December 1899, p. 11. A shortened version of this article (which misidentifies the title of the book as *Morning Glories*) appeared as "A New Richmond in the Literary Arena," *The Colored American* (Washington D.C.), 6 January 1900.

42. "Personal and Society," *The Recorder* (Indianapolis, Indiana), 21 December 1907, p. 4.

43. "When Buying Books!" advertisement, *The Freeman* (Indianapolis, Indiana), 18 December 1909, p. 3.

44. "Another Negro Poet."

45. Advertisement, *The Recorder* (Indianapolis, Indiana), 22 November 1913, p. 6.

46. Advertisement, *The Recorder* (Indianapolis, Indiana), 17 October 1903, p. 4.

47. "Santa Claus' Sleigh Ride," *Echoes of Spring*, p, 21.

48. Aaron Thompson, "Introduction," *Echoes of Spring*, p. vi.

49. "Riley Praises Young Negro Poet."

50. Ibid.

51. James Whitcomb Riley, "Introduction" in Aaron Belford Thompson, *Harvest of Thoughts* (self-published, 1907).

52. "The Party" appeared in several of Dunbar's poetry collections. See for example, Paul Laurence Dunbar, *Majors and Minors* (self-published, 1895), pp. 89–95; Dunbar, *Lyrics of Lowly Life*, pp. 199–208.

53. Sherman, *African-American Poetry of the Nineteenth Century*, p. 10.

54. The 1940 census records that both Priscilla and Clara were educated up through 8th grade. However, the same census entries

report that the sisters were white and that their ages were 42 and 44, respectively. In 1940, Priscilla would have been 68 and Clara would have been about 70. We think it is likely that Priscilla and Clara attended their local country school through 8th grade, but to train as teachers they probably would have relied on educational opportunities in nearby Cincinnati. 1940 United States census, Hamilton County, Ohio, population schedule, Blue Ash, p. 11A (penned), p. 2186 (stamped), enumeration district 31-140, dwelling 229, "Clara Thompson," "Pricella [sic] Thompson," microfilm roll m-t0627-03080, digital image, *Ancestry.com.*

55. Dabney, *Cincinnati's Colored Citizens,* p. 319.

56. Pricilla [sic] Thompson, death certificate.

57. "Emancipation Celebration," *The Cleveland Gazette,* 29 September 1900, p. 2.

58. Anthologized in Shockley, *Afro-American Women Writers, 1746–1933* and Joan R. Sherman, ed., *African-American Poetry: An Anthology, 1773–1927* (Dover, 1997).

59. Priscilla Jane Thompson, *Ethiope Lays,* pp. 25–26. Anthologized in Shockley, *Afro-American Women Writers, 1746–1933.*

60. Priscilla Jane Thompson, *Ethiope Lays,* p. 74. Anthologized in James Melvin Washington, ed., *Conversation with God: Two Centuries of Prayers by African Americans* (HarperCollins Publishers, 1994).

61. Anthologized in Washington, *Conversation with God.*

62. Anthologized in Ajuan Maria Mance, ed., *Before Harlem: An Anthology of African American Literature from the Long Nineteenth Century* (University of Tennessee Press, 2016).

63. Anthologized in Mance, *Before Harlem.*

64. Anthologized in Mance, *Before Harlem.*

65. Priscilla Jane Thompson, *Ethiope Lays,* pp. 84–86. Anthologized in Kevin Young, ed., *African American Poetry: 250 Years of Struggle & Song* (Library of America, 2020).

66. Priscilla Jane Thompson, *Ethiope Lays,* pp. 53–54. Anthologized in Thomas Becknell, ed., *Of Earth and Sky: Spiritual Lessons from Nature* (Augsburg Fortress Publishing, 2001).

67. Joan R. Sherman, ed., *Collected Black Women's Poetry*, Vol. 2 (Oxford University Press, 1988).

68. See, for example, Paula Bernat Bennett, "Rewriting Dunbar: Realism, Black Women Poets, and the Genteel," in Caroline Gebhard and Barbara McCaskill, eds., *Post-Bellum, Pre-Harlem: African American Literature and Culture, 1877–1919* (New York University Press, 2006).

69. Sherman, *African-American Poetry of the Nineteenth Century*, p. 11.

70. "A Casual Review," *The Recorder*, 10 March 1906, p. 1.

71. White and Jackson, *An Anthology of Verse*, p. 233.

72. Shockley, *Afro-American Women Writers, 1746–1933*, p. 305.

73. Dabney, *Cincinnati's Colored Citizens*, p. 320.

74. Clara Ann Thompson, *A Garland of Poems*, p. 9.

75. Anthologized in White and Jackson, *An Anthology of Verse*, and Erlene Stetson, ed., *Black Sister: Poetry by Black American Women, 1746–1980* (Indiana University Press, 1981).

76. Anthologized in White and Jackson, *An Anthology of Verse;* Stetson, *Black Sister;* and Mance, *Before Harlem*.

77. Anthologized in Shockley, *Afro-American Women Writers, 1746–1933*.

78. Anthologized in Washington, *Conversation with God*.

79. Anthologized in Washington, *Conversation with God*.

80. Anthologized in Faith Jaycox, ed., *Ebony Angels: A Collection of African American Poetry and Prose* (Crown Trade Paperbacks, 1996).

81. Anthologized in Washington, *Conversation with God*.

82. Anthologized in Mance, *Before Harlem*.

83. Anthologized in Mance, *Before Harlem*.

84. Anthologized in Mance, *Before Harlem*.

85. Sherman, *Collected Black Women's Poetry*.

86. Boelcskevy, *Clara Ann Thompson, J. Pauline Smith, Mazie Earhart Clark*.

87. Nikki Grimes, *One Last Word: Wisdom from the Harlem Renaissance* (Bloomsbury, 2017).

88. Sherman, *Collected Black Women's Poetry*, p. xxxiv.

89. White and Jackson, *An Anthology of Verse,* pp. 232–233.

90. Ibid., p. 233.

91. Clara Ann Thompson, Foreword to *A Garland of Poems,* p. 9.

92. Clara Ann Thompson, "What Means This Bleating of the Sheep?" *A Garland of Poems,* pp. 78–79.

93. Ibid., 82.

94. "Personal," *The Union* (Cincinnati, Ohio), 30 September 1922, p. 2.

95. Clara Ann Thompson, "Our Side of the Race Problem," *A Garland of Poems,* p. 84.

Wesley R. Bishop is an assistant professor of American history at Marian University Indianapolis. His current research examines the influences of turn of the century protest politics on modern American political thought. He is a member of the Society for the Study of Midwestern Literature and the Labor and Working Class History Association. He lives in northern Indianapolis and is the managing editor of *The North Meridian Review: A Journal of Culture and Scholarship.*

Patricia Oman is an associate professor of English at Hastings College (Hastings, Nebraska) and the director of Hastings College Press. Her research focuses on literary recovery and the Midwest in literature, film, and popular culture. Her essays have been published in many journals, including *Cinema Journal, MidAmerica,* and *The Middle West Review.*

NOTES ON EDITING

Patricia Oman

The purpose of this book is to introduce three forgotten, early twentieth-century poets—Aaron Belford Thompson, Priscilla Jane Thompson, and Clara Ann Thompson—to contemporary readers. Collected here are volumes of poetry the poets self-published in the period 1907–1908. Hastings College Press's goal in republishing texts is usually to present them as identically as possible to the original published editions. For most titles in our "Forgotten Texts" series, although we update the visual design and layout, the only changes we make to the text itself are corrections of obvious editor or compositor errors we find during the proofreading process. The Thompsons' volumes contain more errors than we typically find in previously published texts, so we had to think carefully about our publication strategy. Discussions among press staff centered on two questions:

First, does the text need to be edited? There are scholarly benefits to maintaining the text of the original, self-published editions, even if they contain errors in punctuation and spelling. As the introduction notes, however, critics and scholars have not been kind about these errors in the Thompsons' books. By reproducing them in a new edition, would we help or hurt the authors?

Second, what kind of editing does the text need? When a text needs more than a simple proofread, HC Press chooses between textual editing and copyediting. These two general methods of editing serve different purposes. Textual editors address issues such as textual authority and author intent, and sometimes provide contextual annotations to aid readers. We would choose this method if there were conflicting editions of a text, we had reason to suspect that the publisher of an existing edition strayed significantly from the author's vision, or readers might benefit from annotations. Copyeditors, however, try to present the author's text in the best possible light by correcting grammatical and spelling errors, verifying factual details, and making the style consistent. We would choose this method of editing when publishing a book from the author's original manuscript (i.e., the book has never been published and therefore has never been professionally copyedited). The self-published volumes of the Thompson siblings fall in between these categories.

Because the original editions are not lost—resourceful readers can find digital facsimiles through their local or school libraries—I answered yes to the first question. If our goal is to bring attention to the Thompson poets, we should at least polish up the more obvious errors to show the poets in their best light. The occasional typographic error should not distract readers from the poems themselves. I was unsure about the second question until I examined the Thompsons' other poetry collections. Many of the poems included in this edition appeared in more than one volume. After comparing poems across collections, I am confident that many of the spelling and punctuation errors in our source texts were accidental, that is, they do not represent the authors' intentions.[1]

Ultimately I chose a cross between textual editing and copyediting for this volume (a form of "copy-text editing"). I edited the text very lightly for punctuation and typographical errors, but I consulted alternate editions whenever possible. This is not the most popular form of editing among scholars today—I can hear the objections already—but I think it is the right choice for this project. My goal was not to create the "perfect" or authoritative version of the Thompsons' poems, but rather to smooth over distracting typographical errors in the original editions that might prevent readers from giving the poems a chance. There are pros and cons to any editorial approach, though, so I invite readers to join me in thinking through these editorial decisions.

I kept in mind the following principles as I edited: (1) Any editorial decision, however small, has the potential to change how readers interact with a text. (2) Poetry is not just a textual medium, but also an aural and performative one. (3) Rhythm and meter are just as important to a poem as spelling and grammar. (4) Spelling and grammar errors are determined by convention *and* context. (5) These poems belong to the Thompsons. The biggest danger in editing their poems was misinterpreting their linguistic choices and imposing on them my own cultural assumptions about langauge. My general approach to editing the Thompsons' poems was therefore to do no harm, or, when I could not avoid intervening, to do as little harm as possible.

The Thompson poets lived and wrote in a complex linguistic environment. Even though they were raised in an overwhelmingly rural and racially white area of Ohio, Rossmoyne was located just outside Cincinnati. As a growing northern city close to the Mason-Dixon line, Cincinnati was a hub in the latter half of the nineteenth century for both immigrants and formerly enslaved people. The Thompsons would have encountered many varieties of English on a daily basis, and these varieties are represented in their poetry. Further, the Thompsons' poetry indicates that they read widely. Priscilla's poems, for instance, include several allusions to nineteenth-century romances such as Charlotte Brontë's 1847 novel *Jane Eyre* and Walter Scott's 1819 novel *Ivanhoe*. The title of Clara's collection refers to Henry Wadsworth Longfellow's 1863 book of poetry *Tales from a Wayside Inn*. Aaron explicitly likened himself to James Whitcomb Riley, who was famous for writing in Indiana vernaculars. And all three siblings wrote poems using the conventions of "dialect poetry," an American literary genre that arose in the late nineteenth century to represent regional, class, and racial vernaculars.

I was careful, therefore, not to question the Thompsons' linguistic choices. I focused primarily on typographical errors, or what textual scholars call "accidentals." Distinguishing between linguistic choices and accidentals was not always easy, though.

Stanzas, Line Breaks, and Meter

I made no changes to the organization or structure of the poems. The poems remain in the order in which they appeared in the authors' original editions, and, for the most part, with the original stanza breaks and line indents. Because the spacing in the original editions is somewhat inconsistent, I had trouble interpreting line indents in a few cases. I can only hope I did not introduce any errors. Intentional changes in line indent are noted in the text with an asterisk (*) at the end of the line. I changed the meter in only two lines (p. 73, line 15 and p. 97, line 1).

Punctuation

Changes to punctuation were few, but for legibility I did not indicate those in the text.

In *The Copyeditor's Handbook,* Amy Einsohn and Marilyn Schwartz identify four different approaches to punctuation: (1) aural, (2) visual, (3) syntactic, and (4) idiosyncratic. Writers who punctuate aurally focus on the spoken or performed quality of a text, placing punctuation where there are natural pauses in speech or where it "sounds right." Visual punctuators add or delete punctuation based on the "look" of the text. In syntactic punctuation—the choice of most copyeditors—sentences are punctuated according to syntactic phrases and logic. Idiosyncratic punctuators are inconsistent in their placement of punctuation, moving back and forth between aural, visual, and syntactic approaches.[2]

The Thompson siblings differ in their approaches to punctuation. Clara punctuates according to syntax, whereas Aaron punctuates idiosyncratically. In some of Aaron's poems, commas seem to indicate a pause in speaking, but in others commas seem to be placed visually or randomly. Semicolons are also used in some places in ways that do not make sense in terms of speech or syntax.

Keeping a light touch, I changed punctuation only in cases where the syntax of a sentence was obscured (e.g., a comma at the end of an enjambed line). I did not change an author's preference for open punctuation (i.e., minimal punctuation) or closed punctuation (i.e., excessive punctuation). In Aaron's poem "A Bright Reflection" (3–4), for instance, I deleted the comma at the end of the first line:

Original
Oft to my **recollection**,
Drifts in a bright reflection;
And it comes from a direction,
Where all is filled with cheer:
From wood-land dale and fallow,
From brooklets deep and shallow;
And the notes of feathered songsters
Come drifting to mine ear. (lines 1–8)

Edited
Oft to my **recollection**
Drifts in a bright reflection;
And it comes from a direction,
Where all is filled with cheer:
From wood-land dale and fallow,
From brooklets deep and shallow;
And the notes of feathered songsters
Come drifting to mine ear. (lines 1–8)

The comma in the original is based on aural punctuation (a pause in speech), not syntactic punctuation. The prepositional phrase "in to my recollection" is broken up by the comma at the end of line 1. If we rewrote this sentence with the subject first, it would read, "A bright reflection oft drifts into my recollection." Deleting the comma at the end of line 1 is consistent with the formal register of the poem and with lines 7–8, which are punctuated syntactically, not aurally.

In other cases, I changed punctuation for consistency within a poem. In "After the Honeymoon" (85–87), for instance, I standardized the punctuation in this refrain:

> Exposein' myse'f in the slush an' col',
> I wouldn't go to work to save yo' soul.

This refrain is repeated eleven times in the poem, but the punctuation varies from stanza to stanza in the original edition. It is possible that by standardizing the punctuation here I am erasing documentation of the poet's performative style or his attempt to represent spoken (or sung) English. I could not find another edition of this poem for comparison, so I opted for consistency within the poem and gave priority to syntax and clear meaning. (In this poem I also standardized the word "myse'f," which appeared in some stanzas as "mys'f.") Is this a case in which I may have obscured the author's linguistic or poetic choice?

I made similar editorial decisions with regard to apostrophes in contractions. In some poems in Aaron's original edition, apostrophes are not used to indicate contractions in formal or poetic diction. This could be an intentional choice to distinguish between poetic license in formal or "standard" English and colloquial diction in regional dialect, but he is not consistent on this issue. And in some dialect poems, apostrophes are sometimes misplaced. I have therefore added apostrophes to every contraction in the appropriate place, regardless of the dialect or register. Examples from Aaron's first poem, "A Bright Reflection" (3), include

> **'Neath** spreading boughs of oak-wood, (line 11)

and

> **'Mong** vines and leaves o'er head: (line 12)

(Two notable exceptions are the contractions "aint" and "kaint," which Aaron consistently spells without an apostrophe. I have not changed his preference.)

Other silent revisions include correcting the placement of quotation marks in direct speech. In Priscilla's poem "The Favorite Slave's Story" (152–162), for instance, the original version includes quotation marks around an example of indirect speech by a character named Miss Nancy:

> **Original**
> One mawnin', jest to pick a fuss,
> She said she missed a pie;
> When Mammy said dey all was tha,
> She said, she told a lie.
>
> '**Dat** pie was in her cabin, hid;
> She wus a vixen, bold;
> An' ef she didn't bring it back,
> She'd have her whooped an' **sold**.' (lines 149–156)

The single quotation marks here are supposed to represent what Miss Nancy said, but this is not an example of direct speech. If it were direct speech, the stanza would read, "Dat pie **is** in **yo'** cabin, hid; / **You are** a vixen, bold," and so on. The pronouns and verb tense indicate that Miss Nancy's speech is being represented indirectly. My choices in this case were to delete the quotation marks or change the pronouns and verb tenses. Neither is a perfect solution, but deleting the quotation marks is the least invasive option. I added a colon to the end of the previous stanza to indicate that what followed was the "lie."

Edited

One mawnin', jest to pick a fuss,
She said she missed a pie;
When Mammy said dey all was tha,
She said, she told a **lie:**

Dat pie was in her cabin, hid;
She wus a vixen, bold;
An' ef she didn't bring it back,
She'd have her whooped an' **sold.**

Spelling and Homophones

The only substantive changes I made to the text were obvious printer's or spelling errors that could be corrected without changing the meter of the line or the rhyme patterns of the poem. Further, any corrections had to be consistent with the poem's linguistic register (e.g., formal or vernacular) and dialect (e.g., standard or regional). In some cases, I made the spelling of a word (such as a proper noun) consistent within the same poem but did not try to impose consistent spelling across poems or collections. Whenever possible, I compared contested words and phrases with other printed editions of the poem. Changes to words are indicated in the text by square brackets and listed in Appendix A. Editing Corrections (269–284).

The most common corrections were to obvious misspellings and mixed-up homophones. For example, "floocks" of sheep in Aaron's poem "A Christmas Carol" (20) should clearly be "flocks" (line 2). Similarly, the phrase "Ethiope miad" in "Our Girls" (28) should be "Ethiope maid" (line 1). In "The Traveler's Dream" (82–84), I am confident that "**There** odor and fragrance so sweet" should be "**Their** odor and fragrance so sweet" (line 32). When I was not confident in changing a word or phrase or when a correction would change the meter or rhyme patterns of the poem, I did not make the change. For instance, in Aaron's "A Deserted Homestead" (39–41) I kept the phrase "the old planter's **lost**" (line 58) to maintain the exact rhymes in that stanza even though "the old planter's **loss**" would make more sense.

One difficult example was the first line of Aaron's "When Johnson's Ban' Comes 'Long" (97–100), which originally read, "Come out **hear** boys an' lis'en!" Maybe the speaker of the poem might confuse the homophones "hear" and "here" in writing, but dialect poems usually emphasize speech. This is indicated by the speaker directly addressing someone, in this case "boys." In the poem's vernacular, there does not seem to be a difference in the pronunciation of the words "here" and "hear," so maybe it is safe to change the spelling of this word. However, the poem is generally in ballad verse and the scansion of this line suggests that the word "hear" should be pronounced with two syllables.

Come out | **he'ar** | boys an' | lis'en!

Is this a case of a mixed-up homophone or a missing apostrophe? Based on the meter of the poem, I think the latter (though the scansion of the next line is problematic, too). The corrected line now reads, "Come out **he'ar** boys an' lis'en!"

Verbs

I puzzled over many instances of verb tense inconsistency and subject-verb disagreement. In dialect poems, which approximate spoken and regional language, variety in syntax is not a problem, so there is no reason to standardize it. In formal or "standard" English, disagreements in number between the subject and verb can be very distracting, as can be shifts in verb tense. However, some of Aaron's and Priscilla's poems meld formal and vernacular English and in those cases I could not tell which rules, if any, should apply. Given the linguistic variety of their poems, I think changing verb tenses or subject number would be too invasive to the poems, even if some instances are likely typographical errors. I have therefore not made any changes to verbs or their subjects, but I invite readers to consider some specific examples:

In Aaron's poem "Emancipation" (44–45), the line "Our **fetters** long **has** been destroyed" (line 3) uses a singular verb with a plural subject. According to the rules of subject-verb agreement, the line should read "Our **fetters** long **have** been destroyed" (line 3). The poem is not written in dialect or vernacular, so it seems to me this must be a mistake. The subject-verb disagreement in line 3 is not consistent with the formal tone of the rest of the poem: "Three cheers! well may we shout with joy, / and hail Emancipation;" (lines 1–2). Further suggesting that this subject-verb disagreement is just a mistake, in the version that appeared in Aaron's earlier collection *Morning Songs*, the line appeared as, "Our **fetters** long **have** been destroyed."

Another interesting example is the phrase "Yet my **path have** been laid" (line 31) from Aaron's "The Traveler's Dream" (82–84). In the earlier collection *Morning Songs*, this line reads, "Yet my **path hath** been laid." It is easy to see how the error occurred from one collection to the next, as Aaron changed the more formal "hath" to the less formal "have." Even so, I was not comfortable introducing a potential change to the poem's diction.

There are many examples of subject-verb disagreement in Priscilla's poems, as well. In the first poem in the collection, "Athelstane" (109), for instance, "**Is** not thy **hopes** yet blasted?" (line 3) would in "standard" English be "**Are** not thy **hopes** yet blasted?" And, in "A Little Wren" (180), the line "And his little **feet was** hid in the snow" (line 2) would be corrected in "standard" English as, "And his little **feet were** hid in the snow." But Priscilla's poems tend to be more linguistically adventurous and nuanced than those of her siblings—are these poems meant to be in "standard" English? Are these mistakes or linguistic choices?

Priscilla's narrative poems "The Fugitive" (111–113) and "The Husband's Return" (120–123) both contain many shifts in verb tense that caused me pause. On the one hand, I could not think of solutions that would leave the meter or rhyme scheme unchanged. On the other hand, and more importantly, the shifts in verb tense could be significant to the subjects of the poems. "The Fugitive," for instance, is a narrative poem about an enslaved man who escapes to Canada. It begins in the present tense:

> With bleeding back, from tyrant's lash,
> A fleet-foot slave **has sped**,
> All frantic, past his humble hut,
> And **seeks** the wood instead. (lines 1–4)

The use of the past participle ("has sped") in the second line is a little awkward with the present tense verb in the fourth line ("seeks"), but it gives the poem a feeling of beginning *in medias res*. This is clever because it drops the reader directly into the character's plight. The verb tense switches several times after this, however:

> He fiercely **pressed** that day, (line 14)
> He **wades** waist-deep, unto a tree, (line 19)
> But Providence … **Looked** down upon that slave.
> (lines 29–30)
> Till after many a restless day … His haven **looms** in
>   sight. (lines 45–48)
> His tired feet **press** Canadian shore. (line 49)
> With grateful heart he **journeyed** through (line 59)

These changes in verb tense could indicate a lack of narrative control, but they could also be intentional. Maybe they are supposed to represent the emotional turmoil of a slave running for freedom, for instance. Or maybe the instability in verb tense indicates that the past (i.e., slavery) is never really past. Or maybe meter and rhythm were more important to the author than grammar.

"The Husband's Return," about a former slave returning to a plantation rather than running from it, has a similar issue with verb tense consistency. It starts in the past tense, as readers are told a "golden gleam ... **roused** [the man] from his dream" (lines 2–5). The fourth stanza switches to present tense, though:

> He **now locates** the plundered land,
> Where his young wife must be. (lines 19–20)

According to the persnickety narrative conventions of twentieth-century "standard" English, this switch in tense would be fine if it were the only change in tense in the poem or it were used to indicate a particularly suspenseful moment in the poem's narrative (the historical present tense). However, the poem moves back and forth between past and present:

> He **said**, with rising fear. (line 37)
> He simply **says**, "All slaves are free, (line 43)
> His oaths **are** fierce and wild; (line 47)
> He **loosed** his hold to go. (line 55)
> He **cried** with deadly fear, (line 62)
> Young Stephen's wrath **is** all forgot, (line 81)

And then there are lines in which it is impossible to determine the verb tense:

> The master ... wildly **glare**. (line 28–29)
> He **recognize** the face, (line 32)
> Young Stephen ... His strongest will **employ**; (lines 41–42)

I am not sure what to make of these shifts in verb tense in "The Fugitive" and "The Husband's Return." The poems are not written in dialect, but they do seem to include elements of vernacular language or oral storytelling. While I think some verb tense or number problems are probably errors, it seems best to me to leave well enough alone and let readers make their own assessments.

Conclusion

Reader, did I make the right choices? Is it consistent to edit punctuation and misspellings but not subject-verb disagreements? My goal in editing the Thompsons' poems was to polish them up without changing the authors' linguistic choices. If nothing else, I hope this explanation of my editorial decisions will encourage readers to look closely at the Thompsons' poems. They deserve and reward careful, close attention.

Notes

1. A 1908 article in the Indianapolis newspaper *The Freeman* notes that Aaron's book *Harvest of Thoughts* is "in its third edition." However, we have not found any record or copies of the book marked as a second or third edition. We do not know if the "editions" were printed from the same plates (i.e., different printing runs) or each was typeset from scratch (i.e., different editions). "Indiana's Successful Negro Poet," *The Freeman* (Indianapolis, Indiana), 12 December 1908, p. 2.

2. Amy Einsohn and Marilyn Schwartz, *The Copyeditor's Handbook*, 4th ed. (University of California Press, 2019).

Illustrations by G.T. Haywood

HARVEST OF THOUGHTS

Aaron Belford Thompson

Dedicated to My Beloved Wife

INTRODUCTION
BY
JAMES WHITCOMB RILEY.

It is gratifying to find so much of real poetic worth in these first published verses of Aaron Belford Thompson. Like his racial prototype, Paul Lawrence Dunbar, the gifts of Mr. Thompson seem genuinely native, and give high promise of the young poet's literary future.

— *James Whitcomb Riley.*

A Bright Reflection

Oft to my recollection
Drifts in a bright reflection;
And it comes from a direction,
Where all is filled with cheer:
From wood-land dale and fallow,
From brooklets deep and shallow;
And the notes of featherd songsters
Come drifting to mine ear.

The vernal beechen wild-wood,
The palace of my child-hood;
'Neath spreading boughs of oak-wood,
'Mong vines and leaves o'er head:
I view them o'er and over,
The meadow-fields of clover,
The hills of golden barley,
And sweet cherries ripe and red.

I hear the wood-land ringing,
The wild-bird's noise and singing;
See the watchful squirrel clinging
To some large old ancient tree;
And a host of barefoot boys,
Laden down with childish joys,
Wading brooklets, with their trousers
   'bove the knee.

The cattle on the hill,
Of sweet grass have had their fill,
And beneath the shade stand still,
While others lie;
Their burden and their strife

Is sustenance through life;
Their plague and only torment
   is the fly.

The little lambs at play,
On the hillside far away;
And for fear they'll go astray,
[Their] mothers kind
Follow close and blate aloud
To the little pranking crowd;
And a thought of Christ our shepherd
   comes to mind.

Such joys as we had then
Will return, I know not when;
But the scenes will never blend
From manhood's sight:
The while, with toil and grief,
We bear [life's] burden sheaf,
Oft sweet scenes of happy child-hood
   flash a light.

But a brighter scene than this
Is that sweet land of the Bliss;
And that scene I would not miss,
For wealth or lore;
'Tis the scene o'er Jordan's strand,
It is called Sweet Beaulah Land,
And my soul yearns for its flight,
To that bright shore.

A Message

I heard a sweet message from summer,
    And it came on the pinions of spring,
O'er wood-land, through fallow of red buds,*
    Where rehearsed the first songsters of spring.*

A soft breeze came drifting before it,
    With sweetness that's hard to explain;
And it brought a brightness like sunshine*
    Brings to us, after a rain.*

That message reechoed the wood-land,
    And sounded through valley and hill,
[Descending] it seemed from the tree tops,
    And joined in a song with the rill.

Seemed like the whole universe caught it,
    When the sweet laden breeze drifted by;
The wild bees searched for their honey,
    On wings flew the gay butter fly.

While insects that dwelt in the grasses
    Awoke with a loud merry chant,
And the air was swarming with beetles,
    And the ground was covered with ants.

Across the mead from an orchard,
    There came a moan from a dove;
The muse drew a song from her casket,
    Of pathos with sweet, tender love.

So often I've tried to repeat it,
  When she sings it so sweet in mine ear;
But my hearing grows faint while she's singing,
  And I turn with mine eyes filled with tears.

Beyond the River

Just beyond the brimming river,
    Just beyond the flowing tide,
I have thoughts within me ever,
    Of rare scenes on yonder side.

Days and months and years are fleeting;
    Still that stream is passing on;
Pilgrims, saints, and angels greeting
    Those who just have passed beyond.

We are journeying to that river:
    Some have reached the flowing tide;
Some have crossed to turn no never,
    From the scenes on yonder side.

Some have scarce begun their journey;
    Some have trudged it faint and slow;
Some have reached the topmost mountain,
    Looking on the vale below.

They can see the brimming river,
    How divied her banks between,
Where the parting friends doth sever,
    Ford the tide to realms unseen.

I have dearest friends who've left me,
    And have crossed that whelming flood,
Left their all, their earthly duty,
    And have gone to meet their God,

Where 'tis said, the sun shines ever,
    And the trees forever green,
Where there's grief and parting never,
    Oh! that Beaulah land unseen.

When I've trod life's dreary highway,
    Footsore, weary, lame and slow,
When I've climbed the mountain's summit,
    When I've reached the vale below,

May I cross that brimming river,
    Fearless of its mighty flood,
Leave my earthly cares forever,
    Cross with joy to meet my God.

Lines to Autumn

Jack-Frost has chilled the summer air
    And kissed the flowing rill;
The vernal land-scape hue has gone,
    From wood-land mead and hill.
And ev'ry rustle of the leaves,
    And ev'ry sound we hear,
Seems but to say, from day to day,
    That dreary autumn 's here.
        Oh Autumn! whither comest thou*
            To bind me with a spell?
        A melancholy troubled state,
            Would God that I could tell.

Some trees are clad in yellow robes,
    And some bedecked in brown;
And some have donned a crimson cloak,
    To awe the landscape 'round.
Our high hopes of the future
    Have come to naught at last;
Our brightest dream of springtime
    Have turned back to the past.
        Oh [A]utumn! whither comest thou
            To bind me with a spell?
        A melancholy troubled state,
            Would God that I could tell.

Fleet hounds pursue the rabbit,
    Through underbrush and dell;
The hills send back an echo,
    Caused by their doleful yell;
High up among the giant oaks,
    An echo pierce the sky;

From some old hawk in search of prey,
    There comes a hideous cry.
        Oh Autumn! whither comest thou
            To bind me with a spell?
        A melancholy troubled state,
            Would God that I could tell.

Song-birds, now flying southward,
    Have sang their parting song;
Each one in flight is trying
    To head the pressing throng;
The crows have filled the wild-wood
    With sentinels around,
They feast on seeds and insects,
    From off the fertile ground.
        Oh Autumn! whither comest thou
            To bind me with a spell?
        A melancholy troubled state,
            Would God that I could tell.

I look upon the harvest, in rich abundance yield;
    But still a spell of sadness
Around my soul doth steal;
    To know that once with beauty,
In youthful vigor spread,
    Large fields of blooming clover,
And corn-fields—all are dead.
        Oh Autumn! whither comest thou
            To bind me with a spell?
        A melancholy troubled state,
            Would God that I could tell.

But still my soul feels dreary,
    Although the sun doth shine;
He brings no balm like springtime
    To heal this soul of mine;
And ofttimes how I wonder!
    My outer self seems gay;
My inner soul far down within,
    Each moment seems to say:
        Oh Autumn! whither comest thou
            To bind me with a spell?
        A melancholy troubled state,
            Would God that I could tell.

A Plea to the Muse

Oh Goddess of song, come grant a reflection!
    Unbolt the great doors of memory's wall,
And there let me enter, in gardens, through courtyards,
    And view the great paintings that hang in the hall.
Then grant, at your leisure, some musical measure;
    My harp is untuned and infer'or to thine:
So pledge me one measure, 'twill be of great pleasure;
    Perchance it might soothe this vain yearning of mine.

Then away let me ramble, 'cross brooklets through brambles,
'Cross moorland through fallows,
    To the far distant hill,
Where the century eagle 'mong the cliffs find her hiding,
      And the night winds bring notes
    From the wild whip-poor-will.
She took up her harp, embossed with rare jewels;
    The numberless strings all glittered like gold;
Then a bright glittering [rainbow] [descended] from heaven,
    Surounded the damsel, illuming the whole.

Her jewel decked fingers were active and nimble;
    A bracelet of rubies hung loose from her wrist;
Her dark curly locks had gold in their tresses;
    Her face was so comely, there was nothing amiss.
She scarce touched the strings,
Ere the great harp responded;
    The music was soft yet it echoed afar:

And the sweet chimes came back from wood-land and
    mountain,
    And through the great hall-way, whose door stood
        ajar.

I entered the hall-way and gazed at the paintings,
    Both modern and ancient, magnificent, grand;
My eyes caught the beauty,
Mine ears drank the music
    That came from her harp, and re-echoed the land.
And last, but not least, to the rear of the hall-way,
    There hung a great painting of wonderful cost;
And the muse on her harp played a dirge sweet and
    solemn,
    As I gazed at my crucified Lord on the cross.

His visage though care worn,
Showed love and compassion;
Great nails pierced His hands,
    And like wise, His feet:
Me thought I could hear the wail of the women
    [Descending] the vale of Mt. Calvary's Steep.
Then the muse touched the strings,
And a great song of triumph
Rang out in the hall-way,
    Ere I thought to depart,
While mine eyes caught the sight of a wonderful
    painting
        That brought great rapture and joy to my heart.

'Twas where He had entered
The great gates of Heaven,
And countless the angels about Him did throng;
Here the muse ceased her playing,

For she teared to attempt it,
And she blushed when I asked her
    To join in the song.
As I left the great hall-way,
The door closed behind me;
The muse she had vanished,
    The music had ceased;
I awoke, 'twas a dream—the rain was fast falling,
And the wind shook my lattice,
    That came from the east.

Night

Night on her sable pinions
    Came down at close of day:
She took her flight,
Through the gray twilight,
    And banished the sun away.
Arrayed in her dark sable garments,
    With her jet black [curly] hair,
She paused by the brook,
And a draught she took,
    While a coolness filled the air.

She lay her hand on the reaper,
    Who had tilled and sowed and reaped,
And bade him to lay
From the toils of the day,
    In a restful slumber of sleep.
And going 'cross meadow and valley,
    And seeing things quiet and still,
She paused by the rocks,
And summoned the fox,
    And cried to the wild whip-poor-will.

The wild-fox responded the summon,
    Which came by that of the spright;
And off in the dew,
Through the meadow, he flew,
    And was lost in the gloom of the night.
    The whip-poor-will came from her hiding,
Among the fallows and trees;
    She warbled and sang,
    Till her sweet voice rang,
Like music afloat on the breeze.

Then night drew her dark sable curtain,
    Which parted the light from the day:
That the sun should not mar,
She lit up each star,
    With a gleam from the white milky-way.
All robed in her dark spectral garments,
    Dripping with cold midnight-dew,
She sate in repose,
Till day light arose,
    Then away from the sunlight she flew.

An Ode to Ireland
Written by Request

A song to old Ireland, tho' simple and silly,
I'll sing to the shamrock, I'll sing of the lily;
I'll sing of her sons and her daughters the while,
The lords and the peasants of Emeral' Isle.

Were I but enchanted, I'd rise in the air,
And warble a ditty, beyond all compare,
Of her [warriors] tried, who wielded the [sword],
In that fierce bloody battle of Old Yellow Ford.

In Shannon's sweet waters, I'd glide in my bark,
And chant you a ditty of Dublin and Cork;
Her [chieftains], who headed her men on the field,
The valiant O'Donnels, and dauntless O'Neils.

I'd sing of her bards, but weak is my tongue;
My voice is too faint, and my harp is unstrung;
To sing such a measure, to give them just due,
'Twould be such a [ballad], the world never knew.

So I'll sing of old Erin, a ballad of praise,
Her shamrocks and lilies, her uplands and braes;
A toast and a ballad, to that Isle 'cross the sea;
Long life to her peasants, and lords of degree.

Santa Claus' Sleigh Ride
Dedicated to the Little Ones

'Twas late in the month of December,
    And all things were merry and gay,
When Santa Claus came from his dwelling of fame,
    And took up the [reins] in his sleigh.

Ere he seated, he sounded his bugle,
    In a tone that was cheering and clear;
He then cried out, with a merry old shout,
    To his three score span of deer.

Then away with a loud, merry clatter,
    His bells echoed loud on the wind;
And he with his sleigh was soon far away,
    While his mansion lay far, far behind.

His reindeer were active and nimble,
    They bounded in haste through the snow;
For short was the night, to take such a flight,
    To millions of homes, don't you know.

His stay was short in each dwelling,
    Where the little ones slept in their beds,
And leaving some toys for the girls and the boys,
    He ['gain] mounted roofs overhead.

In some climes the snow had not fallen,
    Then what did Old Santa Claus do?
Why—he yelled to his deer in a voice shrill and clear;
    They ascended the air, and they flew.

And long 'fore it dawned Christmas morning,
    He had made his journey complete;
From his three score deer, he took all the gear
    And piled them, a heap, at his feet.

His good wife then gave him a bumper
    Of claret, all sparkling and strong;
She sang him a health, and she wished him wealth,
    And a life, to be happy and long.

All weary from hasty exertion,
    And a long, long ride in his sleigh,
When the bright dawn did peep, he was sound, sound asleep;
    And that's how he spent Christmas day.

A Christmas Carol

In the fields of Judea near Bethlehem town,
    While shepherds did watch their [flocks] on the
        green,
Behold, from the heavens an angel came down,
    And a bright shining star appeared on the scene.

"Fear not!" said the angel, glad tidings I bring,
    And the glory from heaven in splendor shone
        down;
"In the City of David, this day comes a king;
    He lies in a manger at Bethlehem town."

Then a heavenly host, with harps in their hands,
    Surrounded that angel, a heavenly sight,
Singing—"glory to God, and good will to men,"
    Then ascended in air and was lost from the sight.

The shepherds arose and deserted their fold,
    Went forth to that city, and [Jesus] they found;
They knelt down and praised him, and so we are told,
    From thence they departed, and noised it around.

Yes, His name has been noised from thence to this
    day;
    As we wake from our slumber on bright
        Christmas morn,
The church bells are chiming, our pulses beat gay;
    Earth's mortals rejoice that Jesus is born.

Friendship's Parting

Ofttimes when friend from friend depart,
A new, sweet fondness touch the heart,
   A feeling so sublime.

'Tis but the shaft from cupid's bow,
Which starts love's crimson blood to flow,
   So ends my simple rhyme.

The Chiming Bells

Ho! watchman, from yon belfry tower,
    Ring out those bells to me!
And let my fancies catch the power,
That steals upon my soul each hour,
    While chimes their melody.

I love to hear those chiming bells;
    To me, their music clear,
Time after time, strange stories tell,
And oft they ring the parting knell
    Of friends and kindred dear.

And oft when at the [altar] stood
    The modest bride, the groom,
Sweet echoes filled the vernal wood,
Where giant oaks and elm trees stood,
    While zephyrs shook their plumes.

I love their sweet melodious chime,
    It wakes my sleeping soul;
They bear good news from heavenly clime;
It cheers the heart, uplifts the mind,
    When e'er those bells doth toll.

I love to hear their medley sound
    Swell on the sabbath morn;
Their music from yon tower sinks down
Into my heart with joy profound,
    And banish cares forlorn.

Ofttimes in peace and quiet bliss,
    The raptured music fall.
My soul craves for the parting kiss,
And yearns to break that vale of mist,
    Which binds her like a thrall.

They swell with music sweet and clear,
    Upon each mortal's breast;
Our doom advances near and near,
Those bells shall ring year after year,
    When we are laid to rest.

Ho! watchman, ring those bells to me!
    And let their music fall
With chime, and glee, through land o'er sea,
    In blissful peace to all.

A Proposal

Miss Lucy stop yo' foolin',
    Ah, hush dat geeglin', do!
Say Honey, don't you luv' me,
    De same as I luv' you?
Dis is a serious moment!
    I kum thu ice an' snow;
Miss Lucy won't you hab me?
    Now Honey—don't say "No"!

Yo' mammy, she is willin',
    Yo pappy he is too;
And I—you know I's willin'!
    I leave de res' to you:
Fau you an' me 's been cou'tin',
    Two years, an' maby mo',
Miss Lucy won't you hab me?
    Now Honey—don't say "No"!

Now whut you say about it?
    Miss Lucy, Honey, Dear!
My life would be so happy,
    Ef you wos always near:
Dat answer sounds like music,
    From Luv's Sweet 'Chanted Lan',
Let me stop a bit an' lis'en,
    Let me hold dat little han'!

So Miss Lucy, you've consented,
    Let [yo'] head lean on my bres';
We'll be happy, won't we, Honey?
    I's so gled [you] answered "Yes"!

Think you kin be ready Cristmus,
    I's got nothin' much to buy,
But de furniture on payments;
    You'll be ready? so will I.

A Birthday Tribute

Walking through life's tranquil journey,
    Flowers blooming 'neath her feet,
She has reached each year a [milestone],
    Stationed on life's highway street.

On and on, old time has led her,
    Through the night, and through the day,
In her childhood's joy and sorrows,
    As the [milestones] pass away.

On each one her name is written,
    And life's journey briefly told,
Of her infancy and childhood,
    Written in the purest gold.

And her cup with many a blessing,
    Has been filled from year to year;
She's been blessed with friends and kindreds,
    And a loving father's care.

And a sympathetic mother,
    Who has loved so dear since birth,
Sharing all her pains and sorrows,
    Sharing all her joys and mirth.

She has reached the twentieth milestone,
    'Long her blooming path of life;
She has grown a handsome lady,
    Soon she'll face a nobler strife.

And we've met to pay her homage,
    Friends and kindreds, all around;
'Tis our debt, that we should wish her
    All the joys that can be found.

May life's journey in the future,
    Be more radiant than the past;
And the purest light from Heaven,
    In her pathway, e'er be cast.

Our Girls

A song to the damsel, our Ethiope [maid]!
    Her crisp curly locks, in beauty, arrayed.
Her voice is so gentle, so tender, so true;
    Her smiles glow like sun beams,
Her eyes spark like dew.

Her teeth shine like pearls, her laughter the while,
Reechoes with music, like waves on the Nile;
    Her steps are so gentle, kindhearted is she;
    The Ethiope maid is the damsel for me.

No paints and no powder bedecks her sweet face,
    Her beauty is Nature's, the rarest of grace;
The oils and pomatums ne'er touches her hair,
    Those curled raven locks, by Nature, are there.

Before ev'ry nation, exaultant we'll sing!
Arrayed in her beauty, our [maid] we will bring.

A Barn-Yard Confusion

Marandy, you an' all de chaps
    Come here! you heard me call:
Dis good fah nothin' lazy nag*
    Lay cross-ways in de stall.

A great big pile of skin an' bones
    Done et my oats an' hay;
An' now right here at plowin' time
    He 's gwine to pass away.

Miss Lucy, what's you geeglin' bout?
    You aint too big to whale:
Come hear and grab old Balley's head!
    You Mose, come grab his tail!

Look out dah mammy, watch dem heels!
    We's gwine to turn him 'round;
Now ev'ry body lend a han',
    Let's git him off de ground.

Git up! Git up! you scoundrel beast!
    Push ha'd now, one an' all;
Ah, we kaint hold him! git away,
    An' let the roskul fall.

I have a mind to git my ax,
    An' bust his plagued head;
A good fau nothin' plug like dis
    Is better off when dead.

Now Mose, you go an' git a plank,
    I'm gwine to make a prop;
So when we git him on his feet,
    He kaint in no wise drop.

Git ready now! an' let us try
    To git him on his feet;
Git up! Come up saw! move about!
    You aint too sick to eat.

Be careful when he makes dat lunge,
    An' ketch him 'fo' he fall!
I'll put dis plank against his side,
    And bind him to the stall.

Git up now Baldey! Come up sah!
    Gib me dat buggy spoke!
I brung him to his feet dat time;
    Look out! dat plank 's done broke.

Lay down an' die you scoundrel beast;
    Kaint eat my oats an' hay,
An' think dat you kin take a res',
    By playin' off dis way.

Nex' time I'll buy a better horse,
    One dat is sound an' 'live;
I'm tired of dese two dollah plugs,
    Gwine pay 'bout fo' or five.

The Dreary Day

The clouds creep low, the day is dark,
    The wind howls sad and drear;
The rain descends with glittering spark,
    No cheerful sunlight near.

The orchard trees, their leaves all drenched,
    Bend low their vernal crown;
The fertile soil her thirst has quenched,
    But still the rain comes down.

Oh dreary day! Filled to the brim,
    The brooklet struggles on;
The mist, the fog, so dark, so dim;
    Oh! where has sunlight gone?

That glittering orb once lit the land,
    With splendor, bright and clear;
Through stormy clouds his light grows wan;
    Has nature lost her cheer?

Deep in my melancholy breast,
    There comes a tranquil voice,
A gentle murmur pure and blest,
    Which bids my soul rejoice.

The fair Muse caught the cheering phrase,
    Which sounds like vesper chimes;
Her pen retraced a fiery blaze,
    In feet of rhythmic rhymes.

I read—and in my weary soul,
    The sun has shone again;
No more life's gloom about me roll,
    Though fall the dreary rain.

To Helen

Oh Helen! thou art passing fair,
    With locks of sable hue;
So glossy is thy curly hair,
    Surpass thy beauty few.

Thy smile is like a rainbow tint,
    That lights the sky above;
Deep in my heart has Cupid sent
    A shaft dipped deep with love.

I look upon thy dark brown face,
    Thy laughing eyes I see;
Could I with gifted power but trace
    Thy love in store for me!

Oh Helen! thou art passing fair;
    Thou oft hast heard me sigh,
From wounded love in deep [despair];
    Of thee, heard no reply.

Turn not with modest smiles away,
    Thou little timid dove;
But list unto my plea this day,
    [And] hear my song of love.

Tale of the Haunted Dell

If by chance you should walk down the old dreary
    lane,
    And follow its windings around,
You will come to a spot, that will ne'er be forgot;
    Traditions relate it, believe it or not!
        Where night shades bring sights and queer
            sounds.

Far down in a valley 'twix two wooded hills,
    No wood-man a tree has here fell;
'Tis said when an ax on a tree cometh down,
Hobgoblins and gnomes spring up through the
    ground;
With [fiery] eyes and hideous frown,
    [Defiantly] loud do they yell.

When ever a hunter set foot in that vale,
    With trusty rifle in hand,
He returns with a tale, surpassingly strange;
He talks like a man that's almost deranged;
His walks and habits all are changed;
    And he turns to a curious man.

And many a fisherman ofttimes return,
    From that vale where the brooklets flow,
With a quaint and curious, hideous smile;
Their steps were nimble, their eyes looked wild,
Their knowledge turned back to that of a child
    They had long years ago.

'Tis said [an] old poet once heard of that spot,
    And went, both by day and by night,
Down the old dreary lane,
With a staff for a cane;
His wits were keen and his mind was sane,
    In search for a subject to write.

But when he returned he brought a strange tale,
    He told it in a strange rhyme;
The folks could not tell,
Though the rhythm sound well,
About the strange sights he saw down the dell,
    What he meant, one half of the time.

This troubled the poet, he went back again,
    And roved through the dell as before;
But that night came a storm of thunder and rain;
The people did worry, they looked in vain,
    But the poet was seen no more.

They say that night about the lone cot
    Where the poet had dwelt so long,
Strange faces and sights the people did see;
They sang a strange sweet melody,
    The poet's selfsame song.

One night a stranger entered the town,
    A curious looking old man;
His robes were of a crimson hue,
His dusty feet without a shoe;
His garment skirts were wet with dew,
    His face was dark and tanned.

Around him thronged a curious croud,
    And asked from whence he came;
The pilgrim raised his palsied hand;
It spread a light on ev'ry man;
His voice like thunder shook the land,
    And quivered all the flame.

The Pilgrim's Reply
"I came from yonder haunted dell,"
The aged pilgrim said.
"Into a lonely cave I dwell
    Among dry bones of men,
Once stricken by a dreadful spell,
    While coming down the glen.

"But there is one who lately fell
    A victim in yon glen;
You've missed his foot-steps and his song;
Your hearts are sad, you've mourned him long;
    He was your guide and friend.

"His spirit hovers o'er his bones,
    And will not let me rest.
When e'er I wander from the cave,
I hear him calling from the grave."
Then pushing 'side his long gray beard,
    A scroll took from his breast.

"And so I'll sing his last farewell,
    His spirit 'quest me long."
And when the pilgrim oped the scroll,
'Twas written on twelve sheets of gold,
    But no one caught the song.

A swell of music from afar,
    Chorded with ev'ry line;
Grand was the song the pilgrim sung,
'Twas for the old, 'twas for the young,
    And beings of all kind.

The birds of the wilderness circled in air,
    And lit by the old pilgrim's side;
The wolf and the panther came out from their lair;
They listened in silence: long, long did they stare,
    For no more in fear did they hide.

The ermine and fox came out from the rocks,
    For well they the song understood;
And the old haunted dell was charmed by the spell;
Hobgoblins and gnomes awoke with a yell,
    And wild witches cried in the woods.

The old mountain oaks did nod on the breeze,
    And kept a time with the song;
And dead men 'rose from the roots of the trees,
Who centuries past by the spell were seized,
    And elbowed their way through the throng.

And when he sang of the haunted dell,
    There were parts they could understand.
Said—"There a wood-land witch did dwell;
On ev'ry one she cast a spell,
That wandered through the haunted dell,
    Or wronged her forest land."

[At length] the old pilgrim finished his song;
    Then handing the golden [scroll]
To a strange looking man, who came from the dark,
    He moaned like a dove and sang like a lark;
Together they fled from the throng.

So ends up my tale of the old haunted dell,
    Where witches and hobgoblins stay;
It is still told around that the vale can be found,
If you follow the lane, with its windings around;
    It's some where far, far away.

A Deserted Homestead

Far down in the land of old Dixie,
    Where cane-brake and cotton-fields grow,
I saw there a large plantation,
    Which flourished long years ago:
The cabins, they were deserted,
    The fences, all tumbled down.
All things about me were silent;
    The slaves had deserted, and gone.

As I looked at those rude built cabins,
    On that sad deserted spot,
I thought of my old forefathers,
    And their humble, bitter lot.
I gazed at the large old homestead,
    On her vine clad ruined walls;
It roused within a strange feeling,
    Like the sight of some dead man's pall.
While I passed through the broken down portals,
    And entered the large, spacious halls,
The old doors squeaked on their hinges,
    And saffron stained were the walls.

Far up in the dreary old attic,
    As the winds of autumn did moan,
I thought I could hear a pleading voice,
    Like a bondmaid's helpless groan.
As I entered the large old parlor,
    Once flourished with [southern] grace,
Where oft sat the rich old planter,
    In wealth by that large fireplace,

I saw no trace of existence,
    Where mortals lately had been;
The drifting of time had banished her prime,
    And now shone the wages of sin.

For the power of that wicked old planter,
    Who once bound my fathers in chain,
Had been quelled by the hand of Jehovah,
    Been severed and broken in twain:
In the fierce battle fought at old Shiloh,
    By death-shots from Northern guns,
There fell four bodies all mangled;
    It was the old planter and sons.
They have yielded to dust in the churchyard,
    The mother and daughters lie there;
And the broken down house, all deserted,
    Is now standing silent and bare.

The swallow had built in the chimney,
    The wren had built in the wall,
Through tangled vines and tall grasses,
    The venomous serpent crawls.
The fields where grew the white cotton,
    Where the poor black slaves used to hoe,
Long since they have turned to a fallow;
    There the birch and the cotton-wood grow.
'Twas the Lord that tore down that dwelling,
    And checked that old planter's reign;
Each slave He unyoked from their bondage,
    And bad them to shake off their chain.

How could I look on with compassion,
    And mourn o'er the old planter's lost?
'Twas a just return for his vile, vile deeds,
    And his life-blood and wealth paid the cost.
And leaving the scenes far behind me,
    I returned from that dreary old place,
Whose [grandeur] and splendor had faded,
    The pages of wealth all [erased].

The pages of wealth all erased.

A Serenade

Come, open the window,
    My sweet dusky maid!
And list to my singing,
    A love serenade!
    A love serenade!

There's music and love
    Afloat in the air;
'Tis all on account
    Of a damsel so fair!
    A damsel so fair!

My harp is in tune,
    And my hand is in plight,
But my love-sick heart
    Is a burden to night.
    A burden to night.

Oh! list to my ditty,
    My beautiful Grace,
And show me once more,
    A smile on thy face,
    A smile on thy face.

And oh! what a blessing
    Of joy it would be,
If some day you'd open
    Your heart unto me,
    Your heart unto me.

I'd sing like the song-birds,
    'Mong blossoms of June,
A ballad of love
    To a livelier tune,
    A livelier tune.

Emancipation

Three cheers! well may we shout with joy,
    And hail Emancipation;
Our fetters long has been destroyed:
    We are a free, free nation.

No more like cattle on the hills,
    That feed upon the clover,
Shall wait our brethern for their doom,
    Unable to discover.

No more upon our brother's track
    We'll hear the blood-hounds baying,
The cries of men to bring him back,
    With curse and evil sayings.

No more our maidens bought and sold,
    The southern tyrant's booty;
No more the brutal trader's gold
    Shall buy the sable beauty.

No more our brave and gallant youths
    Shall tremble of tomorrow;
Behold, sweet liberty and truth
    Has broke the chains of sorrow.

For now we stand on freedom's plain,
    With joy and exultation;
Though scarred and maimed,
From bondage chain,
    We'll hail Emancipation.

Three cheers! we'll shout our liberty,
    Long may our nation live;
Large, large may grow her fruitful tree,
    And sweetest manna give.

Miss Susie's Social

Did you hear about the social
    That took place at Susie [Green's]?
That's so! you were off at college:
    Well, you missed one swell old scene.

I was there, and sakes 'o Goodness!
    What a swell old time we had;
Odor steamin' from the kitchen,
    'Nough to drive the hungry mad.

And a mighty crowd of people
    Came a flocking through the door,
Dressed in finest silks an' satins,
    Gals I never seen before.

Brown skin gals with yellah fellahs,
    Yellah gals with brown skin boys,
All a smilin' an' contented:
    For that social they enjoyed.

Lucy Brooks an' Sally Carter,
    'Pon my word, was lookin' fine;
Bet you can't pick out two ladies
    That can take away their shine.

They're the' finest gals, I rec'on,
    Can be found for miles around;
Lucy came with Levy Johnson,
    Sally came with Ely Brown.

Brown, he works for Doctor Collyer,
    Being both about of size;
All the Doctor's cast off clothing
    Falls to him a captured prize.

With Miss Sally hangin' to him,
    I can see that couple yet;
She a han'some yellow lady,
    He so stately: Black as jet.

Close behin' came Levy Johnson,
    An' his face a lookin' light;
Lucy Brooks was hangin' to him.
    She was any thing but white.

Susie Green?—I'd nigh forgot her,
    Dressed to death, an' lookin' gran',
Huggin', kissin' all them ladies,
    Speakin' sweet to every man.

If I'd try to tell all 'bout it,
    Several hours I'm sure 'twould take;
So I'll shorten up my story,
    An' now tell who won the cake.

After payin' pawns with kisses,
    Playin' ev'ry sort o' game,
Aunt Matilda—Susie's mother—
    Smilin', in the parlor came.

In her han' she held a waiter,
    With a cake of 'normous size,
Coated o'er with blood red icin',
    That attracted all the eyes.

"Now," she said, "young men an' ladies,
    Git together two an' two!
An' the couple walks the fines',
    This big cake belongs to you."

Such a scram'lin' then for partners,
    And the couples, formed in line,
Were led off by big Jim Lucus,
    Puttin' on such monkey shines.

Walkin' knock kneed, walkin' jubah,
    Walkin' cripple, walkin' sprung,
And his big cane, filled with ribbons,
    To the lively music swung.

Arthur Brooks an' Sophie Woodson,
    Struttin' to the music's sound,
Made a most delightful figure,
    Following Jim around an' 'round.

Lucy Brooks an' Sally Carter,
    With their partners, was n't slow;
As they walked about so graceful,
    Turnin', smilin', bowin' low.

So between these three fine [couples],
    There arose a mighty test;
And it puzzled all them judges,
    For to tell who walked the best.

But I believe 'twas Levy Johnson,
    He and Lucy won the prize;
Big Man! cut that cake wide open,
    Boasting of its monstrous size.

Soon we had a joke upon them,
    When Miss Carter made it known,
That the cake with blood red icin',
    Was a great big Co'n-Bread-Pone.

After the big laugh was over,
    We all parted from that spree.
What you say?—it must been midnight?
    It was almost half past three.

Were led off by big Jim Lucus.

Boyhood Days

Those good old days of boyhood!
    They've gone to come no more:
When we sat around, as the sun went down,
    'Bout Hen' Clay's grocery store,
And talking o'er the latest news about the country
    folks,
    Or tried to tell the biggest yarn, or crack the
        biggest joke.

Those good old days of boyhood!
    How sweet to me they seem:
I oft look back on my boyhood's track,
    In a melancholy dream,
And view the distant landscape of wooded hills
    around,
    And catch again the merry strain
Of the wild wood's cheerful sound.

Those good old days of boyhood!
    I recollect so well:
Still in mine ear, can plainly hear,
    The chimes of the old school bell;
I see the child like faces,
    Worn by my school mates then;
The girls have grown up to women,
    And the boys have grown to men.

Those good old days of boyhood!
    Are sweet to look upon:
When laughing boys with childish joys,
    We swam in Schenck's Old Pond,

And oft 'mong Cosbey's Pasture Hills,
    In streamlets searched the frog,
Or chased the squirrel up a tree, a rabbit in a log.

Those good old days of boyhood!
    I long for them again:
To scamper and play in the mows of hay,
    And list to the falling rain;
And read about "Jack and his Bean Stalk,"
    Or "Alice in Great Wonder Land,"
And wish to be a wee fairy, or a great big giant man.

Those good old days of boyhood!
    Alas! they've drifted by:
Our old play ground is changed around;
    I breathe a parting sigh,
For here the country people have caught the city air,
    And changed these spots to village lots,
Excepting here and there.

Those good old days of boyhood!
    I will no more repeat:
My heart was glad but [it's] growing sad,
    As those bygone scenes I meet;
Since my barque has drifted 'mong strangers,
    Few, few are the lads that [I know].
I find not the joys I had 'mong the boys,
    In the days long, long ago.

The Bachelor's [Soliloquy]

I care not said the bachelor old,
    I've made no vows to hold me;
I simply tote my hard earned gold,
    And have no wife to scold me.

I've lived a placid life for years,
    Sunshine and gloom commingle;
My cares are small, my wants are few;
    No one to please when single!

No chaps to worry me through life,
    Wrong walks my heart to tingle;
I have no wife, nor family strife,
    Thank God that I am single!

Fritz Mohler's Dream

It was a cold and wintry night,
    The snow fell thick and fast;
All living creatures, far and near,
    Had sheltered from the blast:
Bill [Wickmann's] bar was crowded,
    With loafers [boistrous] loud;
Scott Johnson, with his banjo,
    Made music for the crowd.

"Kum poys und haf von thrink on me!"
    Bill Wickmann shouted loud;
Scott Johnson dropped his banjo,
    And elbowed through the crowd.
The black man sang a health he did,
    To white folks standing ['round];
He knocked a fancy step or two,
    Then quaffed his brandy down.

Scarce had the crowd retreated,
    To card and [billiard] game,
In came a large old German,
    [Fritz] Mohler was his name:
A queer, old looking fellow,
    His head was large and round;
His shoulders stooped, his curled hair gray,
    His voice a husky sound.

He paused to gaze upon the crowd,
    At Johnson who was singing
An old time lively banjo-song,
    Droll rhymes and music ringing.

He sang about the Polly Wogg,
    The snakes, and terapin's habbit;
The June-bug, 'possum, and the 'coon,
    The big-eyed, stub-tailed rabbit.

Sang something 'bout old uncle Gabe,
    Who 'stonished the plantation,
"With pisin vipa's up his sleeves,"
    And other conjurations;
Sang something ['bout] the crow and crane,
    And how he went a kitin',
"Wid his old maustah's span o' mules,
    Way down the road to Bright'n."

Fritz gazed upon the colored man,
    No mirth was in his look—
Until his song had reached the end,
    With laughter Mohler shook:
"Vell poys, let's take a thrink oon dot!
    Dot means faw von und all."
The bottles clanked and each man drank,
    But Scott ignored the call.

"Vell Chonson: call you vonce again;
    Kum up und haf von clas o' shin!
Vot make you in dot courner sthan?
    You look shust like a demperence man:
Be not ashame Got mate you plack,
    Kum valk right quick tis vay!
Dot should n't make your spirit lack,
    All men be mate uf clay.

A vite cow's milk be vite you know;
    A plack cow's milk be shust like shnow;
A plack man's brincibul's der same,
    If he shust thri und keep his name."
Then Johnson took a "pony,"
    And sang a toast along;
Fritz Mohler o'er his lager-beer,
    Sang loud a German Song.

The men all boozed an' jolly,
    The blazing fire agleam,
"Kum poys!" old Mohler shouted,
    "I vish to del my thream!"

The Dream
"Me thream los Tu'stay night, you know,
Dot night der ground vos vite mit shnow.
Each star vos pright, der vin dit plo;
    Dot vos a funny thream!
Me thream ven I vos in mine bet,
Me heard a noisy foot step tret;
Mine hair stood straight upon mine het;
    Dot vos a funny thream!
Me knew it vos a thief, you pet.
But vos too fraid to catch him: yet
Me tiptoed out mine house an' set;
    Und all tis vos a thream.

He valked so easy shust like mouse,
He mate right for mine shicken house;
He pushed dot dour, he mate vun souse;
    Dot vos a funny thream!

Und den me yelled out pretty quick,
Me threw at him a stofe-wood stick;
Und den at me he fired a brick;
    Dot vos a funny thream!

He looked shust like Scott Chonson here,
For den he vos upon me near,
Und den me yelled mit dreadful fear;
    Dot vos a funny thream!
He stole from me tree shickens vite;
He turned an' ran mit all his might;
He shumpt dot vence und crossed der lawn;
Me voke fon day vos shining prite,
    Und found tree of mine shickens gone."

Scott Johnson 'rose with fury,
And shouted, "Look ah heah!
You say I stole dem chickens, sah?
You got to make dat clear!
All night you've flung yo' hints about,
An' now ole man you jes' look out!
Dis sortah talk will nevah do,
Or I will 'pick a crow' wif you;
I did n't steal yo' chickens!"

"Me did n't say you stole tem Scott,
Vot faw you got at me so hot?
A thream be sometimes vot [it's] not;
    Dot vos a funny thream!
I missed mine shickens, dot vos true,
I saw a plack man shust like you,
I voke und vos tree shickens out,
Und dot is all I know about;
    Dot vos a funny thream!

So Chonson, dot vud make you clear,
Kum let us haf a clas of peer!
Me pleve 'tis getin' late me fear;
    Dot only vos a thream!"
And so these two men drank again,
But neither sang a song;
Old Fritz still believe his dream is right,
And Scott still swear 'twas wrong.

Scott Johnson 'rose with fury.

The Same Old Sun

The same old sun is shining,
    That shone in Bethlehem,
That dawned upon the morning,
    When Christ our Saviour came.

His splendor is no brighter,
    His rays are spread the same,
As spread with gold, on the streets of old,
    Where He healed the deaf and lame.

The same old sun is shining,
    That shone on Galilee,
When He called two angling brothers,
    And said: "Lo, follow me!"

While down that dusty highway,
    The same old blazing sun
Shone down upon my Saviour's brow,
    And on Capernaum.

And at the [Jordan] river,
    This sun shone bright and free,
When He to John, who stood amazed,
    Said, "Suffer it to be!"

Through the land of old Judea,
    Through neighboring cities 'round,
Where e'er there went our Savior,
    The same old sun shone down.

The same old sun was shining,
    When He 'fore Pilate stood:
Where sat the false accusers,
    Who yearned to shed his blood.

As they hailed Him king with scoffing,
    Robed Him with purple gown,
The radiant light of the golden sun,
    In silence glittered down.

And on the road to Calvary,
    With thorn wreath on His brow,
The same old sun was shining down,
    That shines upon us now.

But when upon that fatal cross
    The pang of death passed through,
Vile earthquakes shook this sinful earth,
    The sun was hid from view.

And 'round His tomb upon that morn,
    When weeping Mary came,
The sun renewed its brilliant light,
    That glittering orb of flame.

And when an angel rolled the stone,
    And to that mother said,
"He's rose, He's gone to Galilee;
    Come, see where He has [laid]."

Behold! with glittering beams of gold,
    The sun gleamed 'round him then;
"All power is mine," He bravely told.
    "Go, preach my word to men!"

Still shines the same old blazing sun,
    He runs his course each day;
While nations perish one by one,
    He shines upon their clay.

Tale of the Wind

Wind upon thy reckless travel,
    Blowing rubbish to and fro,
Bearing dust and sand and gravel,
    Whence thou come and whither go?
Oft I've heard thee on thy pinions,
    Like the mighty thunders roar;
Saw [huge] trees 'neath thy dominions
    Fall to earth, exist no more.

Thou dost reign upon the mountain,
    On the ocean vast and deep;
Cools the brooklet, cools the fountain,
    Fans the wild flowers in their sleep.
Pause awhile, kind wind, and tell me,
    From what source thou comest, where?
In my songs I'll e'er commend thee,
    Oh, thou Monarch of the Air!

And the wind in martial measure,
    Howling fiercely with a gale,
Thrilled my soul with fear and pleasure,
    As he sang to me this tale.

The Tale
By unknown ways I come to man,
    On crystal wings I fly;
I make a tour through all the land,
    And through the cloudy sky.
Still, still, I hold my secret dear,
    O'er which men marvel so:
From whence I come, and what I am,
    No mortal man shall know.

Sometimes with zephyrs soft and calm,
    Sometimes with breezes warm,
Sometimes midst fragrance from the balm,
    Sometimes a raging storm.
Still, still, I hold my secret dear,
    O'er which men marvel so:
From whence I come, and what I am,
    No mortal man shall know.

Oft I ascend the loftiest height,
    And scale the rocky steep,
Where soars the eagle far from sight,
    Where dwells the mountain sheep.
Still, still, I hold my secret dear,
    O'er which men marvel so:
From whence I come, and what I am,
    No mortal man shall know.

My mighty wings are wondrous strong,
    I frequent every spot;
Earth's fleeting throng has heard me long,
    Yet man he sees me not.
Still, still, I hold my secret dear,
    O'er which men marvel so:
From whence I come, and what I am,
    No mortal man shall know.

Forever on my crystal wings,
    Through bygone years I've flown,
Beyond the birth of earthly things,
    And every man I've known.
Still, still, I hold my secret dear,
    O'er which men marvel so:

From whence I come, and what I am,
    No mortal man shall know.

I've fanned the infant's curly locks,
    Oft kissed the maiden fair.
And far among the cavern rocks,
    Have sought the hermit there.
Still, still, I hold my secret dear,
    O'er which men marvel so:
From whence I come, and what I am,
    No mortal man shall know.

The battles fought in many a clime,
    I've witnessed every fray;
Midst clanking swords and martial chime,
    I've cleared the smoke away.
Still, still, I hold my secret dear,
    O'er which men marvel so:
From whence I come, and what I am,
    No mortal man shall know.

So zealous youth record my song,
    While zephyrs gently blow;
Methink thou hast detained me long;
    On journey I must go.
Still, still, I hold my secret dear,
    O'er which men marvel so:
From whence I come, and what I am,
    No mortal man shall know.

Reason Why I's Happy

Say good people don't you know,
I's gwine 'o marry? coase [it's] so!
I's gwine 'o marry Miss Malindy Ann:
Ha! ha! ha-a-a-a! I's a lucky man.

    Week ago las' Thursday night,
    When the stars were shinin' bright,
    She and I walked han' in han':
    Ha! ha! ha-a-a-a! I's a lucky man.

Had my arm aroun' her waist,
An' she looked up in my face,
Talkin' 'bout our future plan:
Ha! ha! ha-a-a-a! I's a happy man.

    That gal's sho'ly sweet on me,
    Jes' as sweet as sweet can be;
    She is my Malindy Ann:
    Ha! ha! ha-a-a-a! I's a lucky man.

Other boys been callin' 'round,
Tryin' to make her turn me down,
But she tells them: "Git away!"
Ha! ha! ha-a-a-a! I's got the day.

    So good people kaint you see,
    Reason why I's full of glee?
    I's gwine 'o marry Malindy Ann:
    Ha! ha! ha-a-a-a! I's a lucky man.

Down Murray's Hall

Been out all night an' I jes' got back;
I jes' got back from a country ball;
You ought 'o been there to seen it all;
John Lee fiddled an' Jim Cross called;
We had one time down 'o Murray's hall,
    Way down the river road.

The hall was lit up with four big lights,
With four big lights that shone like day;
The whole house seemed as cheerful as May,
For laughter an' frolic had all the sway;
Some joined the dance an' some joined the play,
At the great big ball down Murray's hall,
Where John Lee fiddled an' Jim Cross called,
    Way down the river road.

[There] came a crowd from the West Fork Side,
From the West Fork Side north the river road,
An' old uncle Isaac, to the crowd that rode,
Muttered an' growled how he lost on his load.
He hauled with his mules o'er the river road,
For a [nickel] a head down Murray's hall,
Where John Lee fiddled an' Jim Cross called,
    Way down the river road.

Aunt Jane Hunter came 'cross the field,
Came 'cross the field with her daughters, three,
Jes' like their mammy: but younger, you see,
Modest an' pretty as pretty can be;
A lump clogged my throat when they bowed to me,
At the great big ball down Murray's hall,

Where John Lee fiddled an' Jim Cross called,
    Way down the river road.

How many daughters? there er only three,
There er only three an' they all were there:
Miss Alice the oldest, then comes Miss Marie;
She's one shade brighter than Alice, you see;
Miss Polly 's the darkes' but has the best hair.
They all were down 'o Murray's hall,
Where John Lee fiddled an' Jim Cross called,
    Way down the river road.

Miss Polly, the youngest, had on a waist
Of changeable silk, an' it glittered like gold;
Her long black hair was twisted an' rolled;
Her form was as straight as a straight May pole;
Was belle of the ball down 'o Murray's hall,
Where John Lee fiddled an' Jim Cross called,
    Way down the river road.

Miss Marie was dressed up to taste,
Dressed up to taste an' a lookin' gran';
Had straightened her hair, an' powdered her face,
Had on snow-white slippers, had buckled her waist,
Until its circumf'rence was scarsely a span.
An' she was "Some Punks" down 'o Murray's hall,
Where John Lee fiddled an' Jim Cross called,
    Way down the river road.

Miss Alice was dressed in a lavender gown,
A lavender gown so neatly arranged,
With ribbons an' laces an' pink chiffon;
A golden bracelet she had on,

Where dangled the hearts of the suitors she won,
Who came a foot down 'o Murray's hall,
Where John Lee fiddled an' Jim Cross called,
    Way down the river road.

An' little Sam Tucker was fixed up swell,
Was fixed up swell in his "Swallow-tail";
He toted the cape of Alvina Wells,
An' she is considered the village belle.
Her dress was covered all over with veil;
She walked three feet a head of her trail,
That followed her down 'o Murray's hall,
Where John Lee fiddled an' Jim Cross called,
    Way down the river road.

Abe Lincoln Jones had a Jim-Swinger on,
A long Jim-Swinger that hung low his knees;
The skirts of this garment did soar on the wind,
Like the windy March weather shakes a sheet on a line,
An' his feet jarred the dus' from the chinks in the wall,
As he led off the dance down Murray's hall,
Where John Lee fiddled an' Jim Cross called,
    Way down the river road.

An' John Lee fiddled a plantation reel,
A plantation reel, an' he fiddled it right;
His old time fiddle did moan an' groan,
It woke up the sinews an' limbered the bones;
I tell you: We colored folks danced last night!
The hall fairly shook an' quivered the lights,
At the great big ball down 'o Murray's hall,

Where John Lee fiddled an' Jim Cross called,
    Way down the river road.

That yellow Jim Cross stood up on a stool,
Stood up on a stool, with his back to the wall;
His loud doleful voice rang out through the [hall],
With—"Swing yo' pawtnas!" "Balance all!"
"Fo'ward two!" "An' fo'ward fo'!"
You would laughed at the capers cut on that floo',
If you were down to Murray's hall,
Where John Lee fiddled an' Jim Cross called,
    Way down the river road.

The church folks there were more than a few,
Were more than a few down Murray's hall;
They played more games than I ever knew;
They chose there pawtnas two an' two,
Played—"Run Johnie Willow wind the ball!"
[Still] John Lee fiddled, an' Jim Cross called,
In the upper end of Murray's hall,
    Way down the river road.

I hear the sweet voice of Miss Polly yet,
Of Miss Polly Hunter, who led the play songs;
In spite of the fiddle, her voice could be heard,
As clear an' as sweet as a spring song bird,
Though loud rang the laughter in Murray's hall,
Where John Lee fiddled an' Jim Cross called,
    Way down the river road.

But I'm sleepy now an' I must go on,
I must go on for I'm tired an' sore;
My shoes' too tight, for I danced all night,
My eye-lids are heavy, an' I don't feel right.
I was down to the ball an' I saw it all,
Heard John Lee fiddle an' Jim Cross call.
I'll be 'round to morrow to tell you more.

John Lee fiddled an' Jim Cross called.

The Maiden's Song

I had a dream of my love last night,
When the moon was low and the stars shown bright.
I saw as it seemed, a halo of white
    Encircled a swart damsel fair.

Her voice was so clear and sweet did she sing;
Her fingers danced over each golden string,
As she sang to the time of Cupid's bright dart.
And each note seemed to pierce through my heart,
    But I knew not the song that she sang.

Her teeth were as white as the snow flakes that fall;
Her delicate form was graceful and tall;
Her vesture was purple and curled was her hair;
So sweet was her music that echoed in air,
    But I knew not the song that she sang.

Though she stood at some distance, plain my eyes
    could behold
Her jewels of sapphire, of rubies, and gold;
So gentle and sweet did her tender voice flow;
Her music was sweet, and her music was low,
    But I knew not the song that she sang.

She sang with that ease and melodious grace
Belonging to none but our Ethiope race;
And her dark eyes shone [bright],
With a sweet, calm delight,
    But I knew not the song that she sang.

I asked for the song, at the sweet closing strain;
She smiled with a bow, and sang it again;
So sweet and so soothing her love-song did sound,
And sweeter the notes reechoed around,
    But I knew not the song that she sang.

I looked on the beauty her form [did] embrace,
That angelic smile, on her fair swarthy face;
Enamored, I asked for her heart and her hand.
Embarassed, she fled to a far away land,
    But I knew not the song that she sang.

Life's Procession

They are passing, one by one,
Morning, noon, at set of sun;
When the dawn awakes the day,
When the noontide shadows play,
Fleeting, like the morning dew,
'Neath the golden sunlight's hue,
In the race of life they run;
They are passing, one by one.

They are passing, one by one,
Morning, noon, at set of sun;
Through the sunshine and the shade,
Past the matron and the maid,
Through the vale of death they go;
Through the gloom of bitter woe,
In the race of life they run;
They are passing, one by one.

They are passing, one by one,
Morning, noon, at set of sun;
Men of wisdom, might, and fame,
Princes, paupers, kings the same,
All must meet that solemn fate,
All must pass death's chilling gate,
When life's toilsome race is run;
They are passing, one by one.

My Country Home

Near the highway in a valley,
    Where sweet rose and poppies bloom,
Where cool shade and breezes rally,
    Stands my happy country home.

On her walls, antique and rustic,
    Clings the vernal leafy vines;
In her yard so calm, [majestic],
    Grows the lovely columbines.

Orchard trees, in vernal splendor,
    Shades the grassy carpet green,
And the song birds sing so tender,
    Hidden by the leafy screen.

Calm and peaceful stands the dwelling,
    While great beauty 'round I see,
And [on] my thoughts, with rapture swelling,
    Dawns a trodden path to me.

Dawns a path of thorns and roses,
    Dawns a path of joy and gloom,
Dawns the hour o'er friends most dearest
    Wept I at their burial tomb.

I reflect upon my childhood,
    'Round this cottage oft did play;
Far into the beechen wild-wood,
    Gathered I sweet flowers of May.

And I plucked the precious jewels,
    While this wood-land I did roam,
Wove them into radiant garlands,
    Brought them to my country home.

Long may stand this little dwelling,
    She has harbored me since birth;
Though the hue fades in her dotage,
    'Tis my dearest home on earth.

The Foresight

Behold, the time advances,
    [It's] nearing day by day;
And I view a gleam of sunlight,
    Through a mist and stormy way.
The hour is fast approaching,
    As the Book of Truth record,
When the hand of Ethiopia
    Shall [wield] her trusty sword.

Not with stern and brutal sovern,
    Not with blood-stained hands of might,
But in freedom's name she'll govern,
    With justice, truth, and right.
Oft Caucasia's tongues deride us,
    In their 'tempt to make us fall,
But God who loves His children,
    Looks upon us one and all.

And through His precious [promise],
    Like a dark and misty [veil],
Behold, a ship comes sailing,
    With rainbow-tinted sails.

The pilot at his rudder,
    With cold and bleeding hand,
Long stood with fear and trembling,
    While lost upon the strand.
And oft he lowered the anchor,
    At night fall on the deep,
Or when the storms were raging,
    His faithful watch did keep.

Through the darkest fog before him,
    Which [veils] the light before,
He stands the howling tempest,
    And looks for yonder shore.
Across the stormy waters,
    The winds come down with might,
Ere long the pilot on that ship
    Shall see a gleaming light.

The dawn of day advances,
    'Twill calm the rolling sea,
Like the Hand that calmed the tempest,
    On the lake of Galilee.

I view her in my vision;
    Her shipmates and her crew,
With trusty hopes, are waiting,
    To anchor at yon view;
Though many a gallant shipmate,
    Who were drowned in the dreadful deep,
Lay [buried] 'neath the waters;
    In an aqueous grave they sleep.

I see one brave old sailor,
    Who has climbed the topmost mast,
And he shouts with loud, Hosanna,
    At the scenes before him cast.
She's heading for yon harbor,
    Her sails are now unfurled,
Though drenched, and shaken by the wind,
    Her splendor awes the world.

There dawns another vision,
    And the muses bid me write:
I see her in the harbor,
    Her sails are sparkling bright.

I see Queen Ethiopia,
    Before all nations stand;
She is robed in royal purple,
    And a seal is in her hand.
As she lifts her hand with jewels,
    And takes the solemn vow,
Kings, prince, and nobles hail her,
    All nations 'fore her bow.

Lead Me

Lead me oh, my blest Redeemer,
    Ere my feet shall walk astray;
Through this world of dire temptation,
    Lead me on the Heavenly way.
Lead me, though my steps should falter,
    As I journey through this land;
When I meet with worldy conflicts,
    Grasp me tighter by the hand.

On the verge of earth's temptation,
    When my strength is almost gone,
Haste before I fall, dear Savior,
    Grasp my hand and lead me on!
In my earthly joys and sorrows,
    Let me not forget the way!
For too soon may dawn the morrow,
    Should my steps be led astray.

A Congratulation

Whut brung you from Virginger?
    An' when did you git back?
I's glad to see you, Moses,
    Sho I am, an' dat's a fact;
An' how is I a gittin' 'long?
    I thought I heard you say;
Jes' toler'ble, I thank you;
    Been livin' de same ol' way.

Say! how is ol' Virginger?
    Whut route you say you took,
Down through Culpeppah county?
    I knows huh like a book.*
You found down dah good people;
    An' I 'lowed you would befo',
You see I wasn't lyin';
    Did they hate to see you go?

I kin see you've had good eatens,
    Kaise you's lookin' slick an' stout;
Dem fok'es eat in Virginger,
    An' de grub is nevuh out.
Go 'way boy! now hesh I tell you!
    Talkin' bout dat cracklin' bread,
Go way wid dem greasy chittlins,
    An' dat steamin' soda bread!

You kaint tell me 'bout dat cookin',
    How dem women fry sweet co'n;
Fau you see I know all 'bout it,
    Right down daw I's bred an' bo'n;

Knows all 'bout dat greasy co'n-bread,
    Like a wedge in size an' weight;
When you tech it wid yo' fingas,
    It will crumble in yo' plate.

Dem delicious soda biscuits
    Was de best you evah eat;
An' dat good ol' home-cured bacon,
    An' dem hams, is hard to beat.
In all de homes you tarried,
    In every neighborhood,
You found de young fo'kes clever,
    An' de ole fo'kes kin' an' good.

You nevah seen sich clever fo'kes,
    You say, in all yo' life?
Now, Mose, mind whut I tell you!
    Right down dah pick you a wife!
Gals down daw 's wo'th somethin';
    Dey all kin cook an' sew;
Their han's is not too tender
    To ply 'em to de hoe.

Dey's all de time contented,
    An' never care to roam, except—
Whut's this you tell me?
    You've brung a good wife home?
I thought that you 'd been co'ten,
    By that so'tah sheepish smile;
Hush! you didn't marry Liza,
    Ol' man Sutton's bady chile?

Well I'm beat to hear dat, Moses,
 So I mus' shake han's a new;
Gone an' married Liza Sutton!
 Ha! Ha! Ha! ef dat don't do.
Few [fo'kes] know de [S]utton fam'ly,
 An' their standin' jes like me.
Mark de works I'm 'bout to tell you!
 You done married Quality.

"You done married Quality!"

The Traveler's Dream

In the calm of the noontide when silent the day,
    A traveler sat down for to rest;
He bore in his hand a plat of the way,
    A route that seemed easy and best.
Full of zeal and of valor, this [trav'ler] had come
    Through lands that were rugged and steep,
Midst music of birds, and the wildbees' hum,
    Midst fragrance that rose from the radiant
        blooms,
Through brooklets that flown to the deep.

While footsore and weary he rest 'neath the shade,
    His eyelids soon shut in repose:
In his vision and dream he saw a fair maid,
    Midst [wreaths] of blossoms and rose.
The eyes of the sleeper beheld in that dream,
    With marvel he looked on the sight,
Her raiments, their sheen were purple an' green,
    And her jewels like stars of the night.

She drew near the stranger,
    She stretched forth her hand,
And there did the traveler behold
    A plat with its highways that led to a land,
That land was a city of gold.
But the route was so rugged,
    The hills were so steep,
And the highways were dreary, forlorn;
    There were tombs of travelers,
    In death they did sleep;
There were vines and brambles and thorns.

"Fair damsel," he said to the beautiful maid,
    "Though my travels were rugged and steep,
Yet my path have been laid with flowers and shade,
    [Their] odor and fragrance so sweet.
The end of my journey my eyes can't behold,
    Yet I fain could observe from afar,
Should I look in yon future, a city of gold
    With splendor as bright as a star."

"Arise," said the damsel, "and journey with me;
    And soon on your pathway we'll find
That the fruits of your toil through sunshine and shade
    Lead not to a fate so sublime."

He seized her fair hand so they roved through the land,
    'Cross plain, through valley and glen;
And soon in his dream by a chasm did stand,
    Beheld there his fate and his end.
He viewed from the brink as he paused with the maid,
Horrid sights, as he gasped for his breath;
    In that grim, dreary [depth] through darkness and shade,
He beheld an [angel] of death.

His wings were outspread as he soared o'er the dead,
    Where travelers benighted had fell,
And the bones on the waste of that [vale] thick were spread,
    And the grim sights were startling to tell.

The traveler was frightened:
    He groped for her hand,
To retrace o'er the route she had [led];
    All trembling and weary alone he did stand;
He awoke, but the damsel had fled.

He beheld an angel of death.

After the Honeymoon

Look a heah, Marandy! what you say?
Why don't I go to work? an it rainin' this a way?
    Exposein' [myse'f] in the slush an' col',
    I wouldn't go to work to save yo' soul.

What 'o I care ef the grub is out;
You kin jes go hungry, an' put up without!
Runnin' to the groc'ry sto'e every day,
Burnin' up my vit'ls an' a throwin' it away.
    Exposein' myse'f in the slush an' col',
    I wouldn't go to work to save yo' soul.

I did give you money to buy a pair o' shoes,
I did give you money to pay yo' lodge dues,
An' I give you money to pay the house rent,
You didn't buy a thing! an' the money's all spent.
    Exposein' myse'f in the slush an' col',
    I wouldn't go to work to save yo' soul!

Want 'o buy another dress?—you got one new,
It have n't been more than a week or two;
Oh!—you want one made in a different style;
I'm not gwine 'o buy it, oh no, chile!
    Exposein' myse'f in the slush an' col',
    I wouldn't go to work to save yo' soul!

Did n't say when I 'as co'ten—you know it aint so!—
That I'd work for you in the rain an' snow;
Ef you don't quit a gwine back diggin' up things,
I woont strike a tap till the june-bugs sing!
    Exposein' myse'f in the slush an' col',
    I wouldn't go to work to save yo' soul.

You never put a patch on my workin' clo'es,
You don't give a cent how yo' husband goes;
Jes so he's bringin' the dollars in,
Fau you to carry 'round in yo' purse an' spen'.
    Exposein' [myse'f'] in the slush an' col',
    I wouldn't go to work to save yo' soul.

Look heah, Marandy! don't call me a liar,
I'll slap yo' jaws till they burn like fire;
I'm gitin' tired o' takin' sass off o' you,
I'll cut me a hick'ry an' I'll whale yo' too.
    Exposein' myse'f in the slush an' col',
    I wouldn't go to work to save yo' soul!

Expose myse'f, take sick, lay down an' die,
Yo'd ring yo' han's an' hollow an' cry;
'Twould look a heap better ef you wouldn't shed a
    tear:
Kaise you'd have another dawkey less time than a year.
    Exposein' myse'f in the slush an' col',
    I wouldn't go to work to save yo' soul.

I don't want 'o run a great doctor bill,
An' have Willis haulin' me out to Crown Hill;
Ef yo' own dear wife aint bothered 'bout yo',
Look out for yo'se'f! Lo'd knows I do.
    Exposein' myse'f in the slush an' col',
    I wouldn't go to work to save yo' soul.

I'm gitin' tired o' workin' like a mule ev'ry day,
A given you money fau to throw away;
[Here's] another thing want 'o tell you, Miss:

I'll handle my own money after this!
    Exposein' myse'f in the slush an' col',
    I wouldn't go to work to save yo' soul!

I don't care, Marandy, what you say:
I aint gwine 'o work in the rain today;
Pack up an' leave me when ever you choose,
An' git another dawkey to buy your shoes.
    Exposein' myse'f in the slush an' col',
    I wouldn't go to work to save yo' soul.

Farewell to Summer

Farewell to the summer,
    Behold she has fled;*
Her bright vernal foliage
    Are faded and dead;
The hot, golden sunbeams
    Shine brisk through the trees;
The leaves on their pinions
    Descends on the breeze.

Farewell to the summer,
    For autumn is here;
Soon the skies will be cloudy,
    The days dark and drear;
Wild winds, like a deluge,
    Through fields shall descend;
The trees of their beauty
    Must yield to the wind.

Farewell to the summer,
    The birds that are known
For music and beauty,
    Behold they have flown.
The caw of the crow and the cry of the jay
    Resounds through the wood-land
And fields far away.

Farewell to the summer,
    Sad, sad, my refrain;
Her beauty and splendor
    Fades out 'neath the rain;

All cloudy and dreary our days soon shall be,
    And the east winds shall howl,
Over meadow and lea.

Farewell to the summer, 'tis sad to depart;
    Her charms, they have vanished,
Her beauty and art;
      The vines have grown crimson, on walls over
          head,
Sweet odorous blossoms have faded, are dead.

Farewell, oh, sweet summer! long 'fore thy return,
    Sad hearts shall await thee;
For thee, they shall yearn.
    They shall honor thy beauty,
Of days long ago, and yearn for thy coming,
    Through the frost and the snow.

Out Among Um

Say boys! you ought 'o been with me,
    Las' night a week ago;
It won't do you no good to guess,
    Because you does n't know.
I 'as out among the "Upper Tens,"
    The "Upper Crust," the "Creams";
Them Tisdales an' the Overstreets,
    The Hunters an' the Jeems.

I had that bran' new raglan on,
    My patent leather shoes;
That fine broadcloth Prince Albert coat,
    I bought down 'mong the Jews.
An' fumigated, like a rose,
    You know I 'as smellin' sweet:
The white fo'ks turned an' looked around,
    As I swagged down the street.

Of corse I wore my new silk hat,
    That snow-white vest and tie;
An' don't you know, with all that on,
    I hardly could get by.

Why don't you know where Bryants live?
    I thought you lived in town;
[It's] way down old Wes' Seventh Street,
    A [square] this side o' Brown.
Well, any-how they gave a ball,
    An' it was something swell,
'Twas on their daughter 'Lizabeth,
    So lis'en while I tell.

Great Scotts! There was a hundred gals,
    Of almost ev'ry shade;
An' each one dressed her level best,
    It [m]ade me sorter 'fraid.
But soon I shook away my fears,
    An' let "old nerve" walk in,
Just then Miss 'Liza brought to me
    A host of lady friends.

Miss Tisdale and Miss Carter,
    Miss Buckner and Miss Jones;
Miss Artimiscie Martingale,
    And Miss Priscilla Holmes.

Miss Simpson, Effie Lewis,
    Miss Thomas, Susan Gray;
Them high-fa-lutin' Crosley gals,
    An' Miss Leuvata Clay.
I met Miss Mandy Lewis,
    Miss Cora Jackson too;
I met them Dalton sisters,
    Rebecca, May an' Sue.

Met Elder Coleman's daughter,
    That quiet kind o' gal;
I met the Hunter sisters,
    Miss Gracie an' Miss Sal.
I met Miss Emma Overstreet,
    Miss Lucas, Jane Divine;
Miss 'Liza turned an' said to me,
    "These girls are friends of mine."

I chatted freely with them all,
    For they were looking well;
That's why I used them great big words,
    Which I could never spell.

An' such another feast they had,
    I never saw before,
A table filled with every thing,
    And stretched from door to door:
Light-bread an' soda biscuits,
    Caned fruits of ev'ry kind;
Mince pies an' chicken-dumplins,
    An' Elder-berry wine.

Big yallah sweet potatoes,
    Well soaked in 'possum grease;
I wish you could o' witnessed
    The good things at that feast;
Sweet cordial nuts an' candies,
    Good butter-milk an' cream:
You ought 'o seen us colored [fo'ks],
    Around that table teem.

Elder Dawson asked the blessin',
    An' then we all pitched in;
An' what we did to Bryant's grub,
    It was a mighty sin.

With jokes an' merry laughter,
    The house was in a hum;
'Cause ev'ry one invited
    Was more than pleased to come;

Till Jackson Jones, through courtesy,
    Down from his seat did stoop,
To pick up Mandy's napkin,
    An' spilled that bowl of soup.

It landed right on Jackson's head,
    An' how that soup did spatter!
Miss Mandy sprang to save her dress,
The girls cried, "What's the matter?"
    That oyster soup was flyin',
On broadcloth an' on silk.
    Poor Jackson's plight remind me,
Of a fly in butter-milk.

There were oysters down his collar,
    An' soup all in his hair;
His party suit was ruined,
    I could see it then an' there.

Mrs. Bryant an' the waiters
    Tried to make the blunder straight;
I could n't eat another thing
    That laid upon my plate;
I was so choked with laughter,
    I could n't look around;
An' lookin' solemn in my plate,
    My face put on a frown.

Poor Jackson's head was scalded,
    An' his eyes was lookin' red;
For you see, that big bowl bu'sted,
    When it landed on his head.

[At las'] the big feast ended,
    An' the dishes cleared away;
Jim Lewis tuned his fiddle,
    An' how that coon did play!

We danced till almos' mornin',
    I took Miss Tisdale home;
She's goin' to give a party,
    An' told me I must come.

Weep Not

Weep not for childhood's happy years,
    Grieve not 'cause time rolls on;
Renew the smile and dry the tears,
    And let bygones be gone.
Life's but a day: Though come what may,
    Joy is the birth of sorrow,
And oft sad hearts from grief departs,
    When dawns the final morrow.

Weep not for childhood's happy years,
    Let future come what may!
If life be long, earth's passing throng
    Will find us bent and gray.
Life's but a day: Though come what may,
    Joy is the birth of sorrow,
And oft sad hearts from grief departs,
    When dawns the final morrow.

Weep not for childhood's happy years,
    What is to be, let come;
For soon or late, at Heaven's Great Gate,
    Our journey will be done.
Life's but a day: Though come what may,
    Joy is the birth of sorrow,
And oft sad hearts from grief departs,
    When dawns the final morrow.

Quit Yo' Gobblin'!

Better quit yo' gobblin', turk'y!
    People's got it in for you.
Don't you know [it's] nigh Thanksgivin'?
    Better hide I tell yo'—sh-o-o!
Needn't go away a struttin',
    I aint bothered: No, not me!
I got somethin' for Thanksgivin',
    Ketched him in a 'Simmon tree.

Tuther night I 'as tired an' sleepy,
    'Roun' the cook stove tried to nap;
Took my pipe an' tried to smoke it,
    Soon it drapped into my lap.
Then I heard Lucindy callin',
    "Sam! Oh, Sam!" she said to me;
"Don't you hear ol' Trail a bawkin'?
    He got somethin' up a tree!"

I jumped up, ran to the thicket,
    By a tree ol' Trailer sat;
Up among the ripe persimmons
    Was a 'possum big an' fat.
Turk'y meat can't cope with 'possum.
    Wan' to know the reason why?
'Possum meat is sweet an' juicy,
    Turk'y meat is tough an' dry.

So you see, ol' mister turk'y,
    I aint bothered an' that's true;
Better hide among the bushes,
    Better git I tell yo'—sh-o-o!

When Johnson's Ban' Comes 'Long

Come out [he'ar] boys an' lis'en!
    Look a comin' up the street!
Jes' lis'en at them cymbals!
    Now aint that music sweet?
Look at those crimson uniforms,
    Aint that a lively song?
There's somethin' doin' on the street,
    When Johnson's ban' comes 'long.

That yellow chap is Mosbey Scott,
    He plays that Great Big Bass;
That's no mistake, he's somethin' hot,
    But my! he makes a face.
Hear Taylor's E-flat Clarinet
    A squealin' on that song?
The young [fo'ks] shout an' the ol' turn out,
    When Johnson's ban' comes 'long.

That foremost chap is Douglas Gray,
    Say, aint he black an' slick?
He's in the fines' trim today,
    Jes' watch him wheel that stick!
He winds it 'round like lightnin',
    An' keeps time with the song;
All kin's o' bus'ness bound to stop,
    When Johnson's ban' comes 'long.

There is Professor Johnson!
    That dawk complexted man
Can play most any music,
    He has the only ban'.

His boys are fine musicans,
    They put life in a song;
All kind o' people throngs the street,
    When Johnson's ban' comes 'long.

That little brown-skin fellow,
    His name is Bert Divine;
He's walkin' nex' to Johnson,
    He plays that cornet fine.
An' Harry Lee, from Tennessee,
    Is doin' nothin' wrong;
Those German ban's "are on the bum,"
    When Johnson's ban' comes 'long.

That boy is ol' man Lewis' son,
    Who plays the piccolo;
An' that is preacher Jackson's boy,
    Who blows the first alto.
That big-eyed coon, with the slide trombone,
    His name is Jerry Strong.
You hear the lates' pop'lar songs,
    When Johnson's ban' comes 'long.

Our girls are sweet on Johnson;
    They say he look so gran';
An' they are right: Bud Johnson is
    A handsome colored man.
The ban' is gettin' ready to play another song;
    'Tis fun to watch the colored fo'ks,
When Johnson's ban' comes 'long.

Look at aunt Susan Thomas,
    With years so far [advance];

Her hair is white as cotton,
    I [b'lieve] she's tryin' to dance.
Old sister Pane forgot her cane,
    So has old uncle John;
You see all kind o' funny sights,
    When Johnson's ban' comes 'long.

Whose mule is that? he's runnin' off!
    It looks like Charley Van's;
He tied him to the water-trough,
    An' followed Johnson's ban'.
That old mule he got frisky,
    When the ban' came thunderin' by;
He upset old Charlie's wagon,
    An' made the ashes fly.

That makes no change with Johnson,
    He lets the music fly;
You hear cake-walks an' ragtimes,
    When [e'er] his ban' goes by.
There is no ban' a goin'
    Can beat them on such songs;
We leave behind our troubled mind,
    When Johnson's ban' comes 'long.

You know that tune they're playin' now?
    [It's] "Way [D]own Dixie Lan'";
That baritone an' tenor horn
    Is surely raisin' san'.
The ban' has got away too far
    To catch distinct the song;
It wakes the easy side o' life,
    When Johnson's ban' comes 'long.

It tickles me to realize
    My people's music skill;
All people bound to 'knowledge,
    Though some it might nigh kill.
An' when they boast of some great ban',
    A playin' jolly songs,
I tell them hold their tongue an' wait,
    Till Johnson's ban' comes 'long.

When Johnson's ban' comes 'long.

Meum et Tuum

Ye living mortal, Death's your fate,
Upon Life's Road his Angel waits;
He waits, your future doom to tell,
Perhaps a Heaven, perhaps a hell;
And should you pass him by this day,
You almost know what he will say.

A Strange Vision

I had a vision in the calm of night,
    When all the air was filled with stillness 'round;
Me thought my soul had broke its earthly thrall,
And stood and gazed upon the dungeon,
    Once in misery dwelt.

Took not its flight to foreign lands at once,
But lingered there about the corpse unseen,
By all the friends who stood around,
With tokens of respect for one no more;
Their weeping tearful eyes
    Paid tribute to the dead.

Then turned my soul from the drear dungeon gates,
And journed [past] a thousand different worlds,
Looked neither left nor right, but journeyed on
Until it reached a river, vast and wide.
It paused upon the stormy banks and gazed beyond,
Beheld [ten thousand] [seraphim] in air;
They sang aloud sweet anthems,
In an unknown tongue, that chorded
With a thousand harps of gold.

Prone was my soul to join that heavenly throng,
But feared to venture, for the billows rolled
And seemed thus to defy its journey o'er,
Until a mighty trumpet pierced the air,
And calmed the angry billows of the tide.
So loud and sweet the music pierced mine ear,
With chants of welcome, anthems loud and strong;
My soul ascended in the air as if on wings,
And took its flight to reach the other side.

But ere it reached the other side I woke,
And found about me stillness of the night;
Around my couch was darkness, all I saw.
I wept—because the vision was not true.

Invocation

Oh gracious Master, just and true,
    With all thy wondrous plan,
Lead us, a [trodden] nation, through
    This dark and stormy land!

Thou who didst hear our father's cry,
    Midst suffering pain and woe,
Who dried the tear-drops from their eye,
    Can guide us as we go.

Let not our hearts with trouble wake,
    And say there is no way;
The hour before the morning break
    Gives little hope of day.

Oh let this be the darkest hour,
    Which [veils] the dawning light;
And let us trust Jehovah's power,
    Till daybreak fades the night.

Good-Night

The sun sinks low into the west.
    The weary toilers hies for rest;
The birds have sheltered in their nest.
        Good-night! good-night.

The hour is calm, the zephyrs still;
    I hear the singing whip-poor-will;
Her music echoes 'mong the hill.
        Good-night! good-night.*

A throng of beetles fill the air;
    The fire-flies' lamp so brilliant glare;
From whence they've flown I know not where.
        Good-night! good-night.

And gazing on this scene I trow,
    At night fall when the sun is low,
The breezes calm, so gently blow.
        Good-night! good-night.

As darkness veils the nightly hour,
    Faint grows the dying daylight's power,
And close the calyx of the flower.
        Good-night! good-night.*

Deep in my heart a small voice say,
    A doom shall fall thee as this day;
And all thy friends shall to thee say,
        Good-night! good-night.

GLEANINGS OF QUIET HOURS

Priscilla Jane Thompson

Dedicated to My Sister and Brothers

In presenting this little volume of poems to the public (mostly of which are closely associated with a proscribed race), the writer's sole and earnest endeavor is to bring to light their real life and character; and if in any of these humble and simple rhymes, a passage or thought may chance prove a medium through which the race may be elevated, or benefited, if only in the private mind of some reader, the writer feels that her efforts is fully repaid.

—*The Authoress*

Athelstane

Oh, Athelstane, the faithful!
    Why linger at my gate?
Is not thy hopes yet blasted?
    I for another wait.

Now hie thee, to yon forest;
    'Tis Clare bids thee depart;
Nay, bow thee not in sorrow,
    To break my bleeding heart!

"Oh Clare, why wed another?
    Thou canst but give thy hand,
Thy heart is in my keeping,
    Were I in foreign land.

"Why tarry here, in bondage,
    When freedom is so nigh?
My steed waits in yon forest,
    And champs his bit to fly.

"Far from thy cruel uncle,
    Thy pining heart shall rest,
In peaceful bliss of Eden,
    Upon thy lover's breast."

Oh, Athelstane, the faithful!
    My heart is thine alone;
No more I'll brook their babble,
    I'll fly with thee, mine own.

The Snow-Flakes

Down, down, in millions, blending,
    The snow-flakes gambol fast;
With eddies gay, descending,
    Hurled by the winter's blast.
Down, down, in millions, blending,
    The shower seems never ending,
    While a white spread is extending,
    From the countless flakes, amassed.

Down, down, in millions blending,
    The snow flakes gambol fast;
Each little drop is wending,
    To a resting place at last.
Down, down, in millions, blending,
    Our God the flakes are sending,
    And a lesson is impending,
    Which blind man fails to grasp.

Down, down, in millions, blending,
    The snow-flakes gambol fast,
In mystic shapes, portending
    God's wisdom great and vast.
Down, down, in millions, blending,
While scholars are contending,
And the sage his wits is bending,
    Unexplained, they drift and pass.

The Fugitive

With bleeding back, from tyrant's lash,
    A fleet-foot slave has sped,
All frantic, past his humble hut,
    And seeks the wood instead.

Once in the woods, his manhood wakes—
    Why stand this bondage, wroth?
With diabolic, reckless heart,
    He turns he to the North.

He flings his crude hat to the ground,
    And face the northern wind;
Fleet in his tracks, the blood-hounds bay,
    He leaves them far behind.

By devious way, 'cross many a stream,
    He fiercely pressed that day,
With deadly oaths for brush or brake,
    That chance to block his way.

Erelong, when kind and soothing night
    Had hushed the strife of man,
He wades waist-deep, unto a tree,
    To rest awhile and plan.

He knows no friends or shelter, kind,
    To soothe his deadly grief.
He only knows, that farther north,
    A slave may find relief.

No lore of book, or college craft,
     Lends cunning to his plan.
Fresh from the tyrant's blasting touch,
     He stands a crude, rough man.

But Providence, with pity, deep,
     Looked down upon that slave.
And mapped a path, up through the South,
     And strength and courage gave.

Sometimes, a friendly fellow-slave,
     Chance spying where he hid,
At night would bring his coarse, rough fare,
     And God speed warmly bid.

And sometimes, when to hunger fierce
     He'd seem almost to yield,
A bird would fall into his clutch,
     A fish would shake his reel.

And when on reaching colder climes,
     A sheep-cote shelter made,
Or, law-abiding Yankee, stern,
     Clandestinely lent aid.

Till after many a restless day,
     And weary, toiling night,
All foot-sore, worn, and tired of limb,
     His haven looms in sight.

His tired feet press Canadian shore,
     Friends tell him he is free;
He feels a craving still to hide.
     It seems it cannot be.

But from suspense and thralldom freed,
    His manhood wakes at last,
And plies he hand and brain with might,
    To mend his ruthless past.

And Providence, in years that came,
    Sent blessings rife, his way,
With grateful heart he journeyed through
    His free, allotted days.

Just How It Happened

Well, I was at the dresser,
    A-prinking at my hair,
When mamma bustled in, and said,
    "Luvenia, Joe's down-stair."

Of course I was all ready,
    But say girls, don't you know?
Just not to seem too anxious,
    I poked, and came down slow.

Well, girls! I felt so funny,
    When I came to the door;
For Joe had on a sober look
    I'd never seen before.

But soon he was all smiling,
    And I felt quite at ease;
Then girls, he caught and gave my hand
    The cutest little squeeze.

I sat down on the sofa,
    And Joe,—he sat so near;
That sober look came back again,
    And girls! I did feel queer.

I said, "You look so sober";
    (For girls, that's not his way;)
And then he laughed so odd, and said,
    He'd felt blue, all that day.

I said, "What is the matter?"
    Says he, "My heart aches so!"
Well girls! I was so got at that,
    I only said, "Oh Joe!"

He slipped his arms around me,
    I understood, you see.
Now girls, what are you giggling 'bout?
    You'd kissed him too, like me!

A Prayer

Oh, Lord! I lift my heart,
    In gratitude, to Thee,
For blessings, manifold,
    Thou hast bestowed on me.

When conflicts raged within,
    Too blinding to express,
Thou pitied my still tongue,
    And soothed my heart to rest.

Keep me within thy care;
    Compel me, to the right;
'Tis sweet to walk with Thee,
    In darkness or in light.

Death and Resurrection

The priests, the elders, and the scribes,
    From council, had adjourned;
And Pilate's proffered sacrifice,
    The mob had promptly spurned.

And up Golgotha's rising slope,
    A boist'ous, cruel band,
With taunts, and jeers, and foul rebuke,
    Leads forth the Son of Man.

Oh, what a scene for human eyes!
    Our Savior, bowed in grief;
And tortured by the very ones
    To whom He brings relief.

Close at His side, a swarthy man,
    Beneath His cross doth bow;
Oh Simon! Ne'er did mortal bend
    To nobler task than thou.

And, on the brow of Calvary,
    With scoffing, and with scorn,
They nailed our Saviour to the cross,
    With diadem of thorn.

'Tis done, and Joseph now has laid
    His body in the tomb;
And none except the guards keep watch,
    Amid the somber gloom.

But what can bar our holy Lord,
    Or cross his wondrous plan?
The stronghold 'bout His lonely tomb
    Shows unbelief of man.

When, to the tomb, the women came,
    In grief, at break of day,
An angel, 'mid an earthquake, vast,
    Had rolled the stone away.

No power within this great domain
    Can stay our mighty King;
Oh grave, where is thy victory,
    Oh death, where is thy sting!

Despite the grave, despite the bar,
    In triumph He hath flown,
And sitteth on the Right of God,
    Joint-ruler of His own.

Adieu, Adieu, Forever

Adieu, you haughty maiden!
    Proud Lydia, adieu;
I will not tarry longer at your side;
My heart now heavy-laden,
    With sorrows made by you,
Never more shall thrall me or satiate your pride;
    Adieu, adieu, forever.

Adieu, you dusky maiden,
    You crafty prude, adieu!
[No more] the sport of narrow mind I'll be;
Ne'er shall my heart awaken,
    To love strains, played by you;
I spurn you from my heart, for a maid of small degree;
    Adieu, adieu, forever.

Adieu, you heartless trifle!
    To dally with my love,
When I humbly laid my whole heart at your feet,
My very soul you'd [rifle].
    Your vain heart you did prove;
Henceforth, for nobler maidens, this outraged heart will seek;
    Adieu, adieu, forever.

The Husband's Return

The Proud, majestic Southern sun
    Let fall a golden gleam;
It flickered through a leafy bower,
And fell aslant a traveler's brow,
    And roused him from his dream.

A finer specimen of man
    Was never cast in clay;
A swarthy Hercules was he,
With that rash intrepidity
    Of manhood's earliest day.

He, an emancipated slave,
    From Rappahanock's side,
Assured by Lincoln's strong decree,
Had journeyed southward, bold and free,
    To claim his stolen bride.

From many a camp of Union men,
    He'd found his rations free;
And by their kindly guiding hand,
He now locates the plundered land,
    Where his young wife must be.

A three hours' tramp 'cross rugged hills—
    Footsore, yet full of life—
Now brings him to the handsome gate,
Where flowers bedeck a mansion great,
    The prison of his wife.

And as he boldly seeks the porch,
　　On entering through the gate,
The master, from his wicker chair,
With grim forebodings, wildly glare,
　　As he his errand 'wait.

Advancing nearer, now at hand,
　　He recognize the face,
The same firm mouth, the flashing eye,
The trouble wrought in days gone by,
　　Comes back with no good grace.

"Well Steve, you scoundrel, what's to pay?"
　　He said, with rising fear.
"You've run away, that is a fact,
I'll have you flogged, and shipped right back,
　　What do you want back here?"

Young Stephen, to keep down his wrath,
　　His strongest will employ;
He simply says, "All slaves are free,
The news is heard where e'er I be;
　　I want my wife and boy."

A white rage lights the planter's face,
　　His oaths are fierce and wild;
He calls on demons from below,
To take him if a will he'd show,
　　To yield the wife and child.

The rash young freedman, with one bound,
　　Had seized his deadly foe,
But Providence sent "second thought";

Before the murderous deed was wrought,
    He loosed his hold to go.

There played about that swarthy youth,
    As he strode down the path,
A threat'ning storm from rights bereft,
That stayed the planter's gasping breath,
    And took away his wrath.

"Stop, Steve! where are you going now?"
    He cried with deadly fear.
"Come, boy, now let me hear your plan,
Come, let us talk as man to man!
    Your wife is happy here."

Young Stephen flung an answer back,
    With fury in his eye,
That suddenly did take his breath,
And paled his face, as if grim death
    Had dropped down from the sky.

"I'm a-goin' to the barracks,
    An' fetch the 'blue-coats' here;
I swear this day I'll claim my wife,
Or you will pay it with your life,
    Long 'fore the night appear."

Swift to the dairy house hard by,
    A summon speeds the while;
A slender girl, with sweet, dark eyes,
Comes quickly forth in glad surprise,
    Dangling a heavy child.

Young Stephen's wrath is all forgot,
    As with a cry of joy,
With kisses sweet and sighs of love,
The bright sun smiling from above,
    He clasps his wife and boy.

And, as he strained them to his breast,
    Where tumult late held sway,
A peace suffused his storm tossed heart,
That bade all gloomy moods depart,
    And lit with joy his way.

While the Choir Sang

The threat'ning clouds of yesternight
    Have sought the western rim;
The peaceful Easter sun beams forth,
    "Glad tidings to all men."

The festooned church is filling fast;
    The frivolous, the gay,
The saint, the sinner mingle free,
    On this triumphant day.

Around the altar decked with flowers,
    Each old saint takes his seat;
The organ swells, the choir breaks forth,
    In cadence full and sweet.

But there, amongst the aged [saints],
    About the altar rail,
A vacant seat, an absent face,
    Bespeaks the same sad tale.

Within a humble, upper room,
    Across the street, near by,
All weak and worn, and racked with pain,
    A faithful soldier lies.

He's felt the galling slav'ry's yoke,
    In days now long since fled;
He's groaned in destitution, sore,
    And felt the need of bread.

But through it all, with child-like faith,
    He's looked up to his God;
And though the billows loudly roared,
    He came across dry-shod.

And now, the crucial test is come,
    For Jordan's bank is near;
He's trusted God at smaller streams,
    Canst he not trust Him here?

The choir bursts forth in classic strains,
    The notes unto him ring;
Though he's not trained in classic lore,
    He knows they praise his King.

His soul hath caught the holy spell;
    Who could doubt such a King?
His fav'rite hymn is on his lips;
    He launches, as he sings:—

"Steal away, steal away, steal away to Jesus;
    Steal away, steal away home,
I aint got long to stay here."

He feels his old wife's lingering clasp,
    He faintly hears her moan,
For Jordan's waves break on his ear,
    And drifts him toward his home.

The choir, in rich crescendo strains,
    In final triumph, chord;
They little dreamed 'twere theirs to launch
    An old saint to his Lord.

Uncle Ike's Holiday

"Well, Uncle Ike! This beats me;
  I don't know what to say:
Last night I took it for a joke,
When of that odd project you spoke,
  To celebrate today.

"I didn't take you for the man,
  Kind as I've been to you,
To leave me in this busy time,
Tomatoes spoiling on my vines,
  To loaf a whole day through.

"I've corn now parching in the field,
  Potatoes yet to dig,
Yet you can walk off in this way,
And leave me in 'a hole' all day,
  Nor do you give a fig.

"You colored folks are cranks for sure;
  Here in this busy week,
To stop a good job, just for fun,
And sport around from sun to sun,—"
  "Stop right dah! Let me speak!

"Dis day is 'Mancipation,
  De day when God, who reigns,
Wid Lincum fah his instrument,
De very jaws ob Sof did rent,
  To bust de slav'ry's chains.

"An' now, wid umble gratwatude,
  I's promised him fah one,

To set aside one day each year,
An' meet my people wid good cheer,
   An' 'joice at whut He's done.

"You say, I'se stopped in busy times.
   I answer in reply,
De 'high hoss' dat I'm on today,
You sot astride, dis very way,
   Jest back here, in July.

"Yo' June grass lay cut in de field,
   De wetter looked like rain,
An' yet you sent me right back home,
An' to yo' surrey hitched yo' roan,
   An' driv off jest de same.

"An' mind you, when I spoke to you,
   'Bout wastein' sich a day,
'Faw Jesus Christ I would not work,
Doe tahment claimed me fah a shirk,'
   Dem aw de words you say.

"I won't say dat; I'll wuk fah God,
   But, mind you dis is true,
Mo' serious time will hab to come,
An' mighty heavy arg'ing done,
   Befo' I'd wuk fah you.

"I s'pose you know whut brung me 'round;
   I want dat 'change,' you know;
I call it wrong to stingy be,
Upon de day when we are free;
   Tank you sah; I must go."

A Home Greeting

A pair of soft, black eyes,
    A velvet, dusky cheek,
A flash of dazzling pearls,
    An Eden for me speak.

And next a soft embrace;
    My eyes drink to their fill,
The tender, liquid depth
    Of orbs that ever thrill.

A long, ecstatic kiss,
    That drowns all earthly strife:
What gift can e'er exceed
    A pure, confiding wife?

Lines to an Old School-House

Dear school of my childhood, thrice dear doth thou
    seem,
Now that thou shalt soon be no more;
    Oh, fresh in my memory, sweet visions gleam,
Reflecting the bright days of yore.
    Those days when we played with our faces abeam,
And manhood and womanhood seemed but a dream.

Thy grove, cool and shady, with maples o'er grown,
    Has sheltered us all, in the past;
We've romped 'neath thy shadows, while bright years
    have flown,
    Too sweet and too pleasant to last.
Dear school of my childhood, with pain in my heart,
I yield to grim progress and see thee depart.

And all of our teachers: how bright in our mind,
    We recall every one, as they came;
Each, like a wise monarch, unselfish and kind,
    Did make our advancement their aim.
Think not that the scholar ne'er valued thy care;
    Thy teachings sank deeper than thou wert aware.

Thy dear grove has sheltered, when life seemed a care,
    And trials have clouded our way.
And oft the young lover and sweet maiden fair
    Have wooed here, where once they did play.
Oh, fresh in our memories e'er wilt thou be,
    Since the skein of our childhood is woven with
        thee!

Dear "Amity," emblem of friendship's pure gold,
    We shall not bemoan thee, as past;
E'en now, like that fabulous phoenix of old,
    From thy ashes, a new school looms vast.
More comely in structure, we view it near by,
    And hail thy successor, with pride in our eye.

We dread not the future, oh "Amity" new,
    What else canst thou do, but succeed?
Thy ancestor's mantle has fallen to you,
    And we know thou'lt supply ev'ry need.
May thy present scholars, and those to enroll,
    Inscribe a good record, upon thy fair scroll.

The Examination

"Look here, Petah! whut's dis here,
    Dat I heard at sistah Brooks',
'Bout you fallin' back dis year,
    In most all uv yo' school books?

"You think me an' pa'll work,
    Keep a lazy scamp in school,
Jest to play, an' prink, an' shirk?
    Ef you do, you ah a fool."

"Oh ma, Mrs. Brooks don't know
    What I do at school each day!"
"'Twan't her dat tole me so,
    I aint 'peatin' whut she say.

"But I heard it, right enough,
    An' I'm b'lievin' uv it, too:
Now, I woont stan' no sich stuff!
    So you know whut you kin do."

"I'm not lagging in my books!
    'Less it be my algebra:
They told stories down to Brooks'—"
    "I'm a-b'lievin' whut dey say.

"Fetch dem books fum dat machine,
    An' my specks, fum off dat she'f,
I'll find out whut all dis mean,
    Gwine to test you fah myse'f.

"Look at me, an' look at pa!
    Nevah spent one day in school;
Brung up undah slav'ry's law,
    White-folks used us fah a tool.

"But jest soon as freedom come,
    Me an' pa made up our minds
To take lessons fum Miss Crum',
    An' she said we jest did fine.

"We wuked days, and studied nights;
    Pa right here can tell de same,
How de lessons we would fight,
    See who'd git the biggest name.

"Doe pa now won't have it so,
    'Tis de fac' jes' ax Miss Jane:
I wus fust,—whether or no,
    Kase I had de strongest brain."

"Sakes o' life, ma! how you blow,
    Kase I once misspelled 'employ.'
Look here Cindy, don't you know?—"
    "Oh, hesh! Let me test dis boy.

"Whut's dis book you's gibbin' me?
    'Spose I keer for allerbay?
A, b, c, and x, y, z;
    Here, boy, put dis book away!

"Learned my letters long ago,
    And I thought you did de same;
Dese new schools beat all I know!
    Don't know you or dem to blame.*

"Bring dat spellin' book to me!
    You don't use dat book no mo'?
'Spec' you ought now, we will see;
    Take yo' place tha' by de do'.

"Now Pete spell me 'domineer';
    Right; now spell me 'gasoline';
Dey's 'too easy,' do I hear?
    Never mind, now spell 'machine'!

"'Mancipate' (set free, to fly);
    Once I craved dat soon an' late."
"M-a-n—c-i si man—ci,
    P-a-t-e, 'Man-ci pate.'"

"'E' cums fus instid uv 'M,'
    Dis here spellin' will not do!"
"Dat's de way you spoke it [to 'im],
    Dat boy's jest as right as you."

"Pa, I wush you'd shet yo' mouf,
    An' quit takin' on, so mean.
Now den, Petah, spell me 'Souf';
    Right,—now spell fah me, 'ravene.'

"Wrong! I knowed you'd miss a sight;
    Dat news' straight I got at Brooks'."
"Ma, I know I spelt that right!"
    "Aint I lookin' on de book?"

"Like as not, de boy is right,
    Cindy, let me see dat word;
Dat word's 'raven'—Sakes o' life!
    Kyah! kyah! kyah! you is a bird."

"Oh shet up! an' act wid sense!
    Ain't gwine test Pete any mo';
You knowed when I fus' commence,
    Dat my eyes wus dim an' so.

"Dat's why I bought dem gold specks,
    Dat you made de man take back;
You won't have me here to vex,
    Always, wid yo' spite an' slack."

"B'lieve Lucindy's gwine to cry;
    Kyah! kyah! kyah! she is a bird!
Makin' out she's gwine to die,
    'Case she mispernounced dat word."

A Christmas Ghost

The Eve of Christmas had arrived;
    The children were in bed,
The clock upon the mantel chimed
    The half-hours as they fled.

Aunt Lucy tip-toed 'bout her work,
    For work she had to do;
I've never seen a Christmas eve
    Bring aught but work,—have you?

And so Aunt Lucy tip-toed 'bout,
    With heart expectant, light:
"'Twould be a shame to wake the babes,
    With Santa 'mos' in sight."

But all at once Aunt Lucy stopped:
    "Laws! Whut's dat thumpin' noise?"
She had good reason to believe
    It wasn't Santa Claus.

And yet, five minutes back, had she
    Not seen on pillows white,
Four little cherubs, wrapped in sleep,
    Most pleasing to the sight?

With busy hands and heavy step,
    Aunt Lucy fairly flew;
Admitting that they were awake,
    She had her work to do.

Next, calls she stern, behind closed door,
    (Too busy to pass through,)
"'Now, whut's dat thumpin' sound I hear?
    Paul Peters, is dat you?

"Phil, Joe, an' Babe, I know is 'sleep,
    An' you, too, ought to be,
Ef you don't git back in dat bed,
    I'll lay you 'cross my knee!"

"But mamma, Santa Claus is come!
    I seed him pattin' Ring.
He's come an' fetched his wife along,—"
    "He aint cum, no sich thing!"

"But ma, he had a dreat big sack,
    They did'nt make no noise,
An' when he set it down, to rest,
    He kissed Miss Santa Claus."

"You hesh yo' mouf, an' git to bed!
    Don't b'lieve a word you say;
Fah none has come into this house,
    But Sis an' mister Clay.

"Nobody axed you whut you seed,
    All bad boys see a sight;
You git in bed, or you will see,
    A whoopin' 'fore 'tis light."

So guilty Paul crept back to bed,
    Most miserable of boys,
For fear she'd tell old Santa Claus,
    And forfeit him his toys.

Yet mamma never "peached" on him,
    For Santa brought a host;
And so he solved the myst'ry thus:
    He merely saw a ghost.

A Valentine

Out of the depths of a heart of love,
    Out of the birth-place of sighs,
Freighted with hope and freighted with fear,
    My all in a valentine, hies.
    Oh, frail little missive
        Of delicate texture,
    Speed thee, on thy journey,
        And give her a lecture!

Fathom her heart, that seems to me, cold,
    Trouble her bosom, as mine.
Let it be mutual, this that I crave,
    Her 'yes' for a valentine.
    Oh, frail little missive,
        In coy Cupid's keeping,
    Oh! speed back a message,
        To set my pulse leaping.

A Tribute to the Bride and Groom

Dear friends, we are gathered together,
    With innocent hearts that are light;
Each face is abeam, and meet doth it seem,
    As there is a wedding tonight.
A wedding! with love and peace in full bloom;
And a sweet, comely bride and an exquisite groom.

Dear friends, we are gathered together,
    And happiness leads us tonight;
  We follow her star, with nothing to mar,
    Through the sweet, dreamy whirl of delight;
And we feel our hearts throb and swell for the room,
To encompass our hopes, for the sweet bride and groom.

May this night's love and contentment,
    For the happy pair, prove to be
A nucleus e'er, to enlarge with each year,
    As their barque drifts out, in life's sea:
And we wish them many returns of the day,
With peace, love, and happiness, as only friends may.

Should sorrows e'er darken their pathway,
    As oft in our lives sorrows will,
  May they turn to the One, to whom millions have come,
    And each heard His sweet words, "Be still."
And may His blest Presence forever find room,
In the pure, sweet abode of the bride and the groom.

Emancipation

'Tis a time for much rejoicing;
    Let each heart be lured away;
Let each tongue, its thanks be voicing
    For Emancipation Day.
Day of victory, day of glory,
For thee, many a field was gory!

Many a time in days now ended,
    Hath our fathers' courage failed;
Patiently their tears they blended,
    Ne'er they to their Maker railed;
Well we know their groans He numbered,
When dominions fell, asundered.

As of old the Red Sea parted,
    And oppressed passed safely through;
Back from North, the bold South started,
    And a fissure wide she drew;
Drew a cleft of Liberty,
Through it, marched our people free.

And, in memory, ever grateful,
    Of the day they reached the shore,
Meet we now, with hearts e'er faithful,
    Joyous that the storm is o'er.
Storm of Torture! May grim Past
Hurl thee down his torrents fast.

Bring your harpers, bring your sages,
    Bid each one the story tell;
Waft it on to future ages,
    Bid descendants learn it well.
Kept it bright in minds now tender,
Teach the young their thanks to render.

Come with hearts all firm united,
    In the union of a race;
With your loyalty well plighted,
    Look your brother in the face.
Stand by him, forsake him never,
God is with us now, forever.

To a Deceased Friend
Written in Memory of Mrs. Polly Dixon

The veil of death hath fallen,
    Loved one, 'twixt thee and me;
Thou art now among the chosen of the Lord;
    With heavenly saints immortal,*
      Enrobed in sanctity,
Thou art chanting with the blest, in sweet accord.

Oh, ever bright thy image
    Is pictured in my heart,
Though autumn after autumn now hath flown;
    But memories still steal o'er me,
      In which thou hast a part,
And I sometimes yearn to rob Death of his own.

Well didst thou keep the promise
    My dying mother craved:
That thou shouldst ever guard her orphan brood;
    Oh, blessed foster-mother!
      Thy tenderest love, thou gav'st;
And thou ever taught me lessons, pure and good.

Oh Death! why rob so early?
    Why snatched thou her, from me,
When I, in wane of childhood, craved her most?
    If longer thou hadst spared her,
      I could ungrudgingly
Permitted her to be unto me lost.

Oh, many times, in blindness,
    Have I stumbled as I tread
The rugged old road, which to me is new;
    And I miss thy warm hand's pressure,
        And I grieve that thou art dead,
While sad, regretful tears mine eyes bedew.

But sleep, beloved mother,
    Why shouldst I grudge thy rest?
For thou indeed hast done the "better part";
    A mother to the orphan,
        Of wives the true and best,
My inmost self can yield thee, with glad heart.

An Afternoon Gossip

Is that you sistah Harris?
    I knowed you when you knocked;
Jest keep right on a-pushing,
    The ole door isn't locked!

Ole white man's been forgetting,
    Each day since first I sent;
He's got a pow'ful mem'ry,
    When comes the time for rent.

Now, sit down; whut's your hurry?
    You have no work to do;
I'm mos' done with my i'ning;
    You always beats me through.

You aint no bother to me!
    Jest sit here where [it's] cool;
Hush fretting 'bout them child'en!
    You know they're safe in school.

Now, whut's the news, Amanda?
    Hearn some 'bout Flora Ann;
Jest take this little rocker,
    And reach that pa'm leaf fan.

I hearn she's gone and married
    That trifling Louis Bird;
Says I to Abe this mo'nin',
    Don't b'lieve a single word.

Hush, woman! Whut's you sayin'?
    How can that news be true?
Flo Ann wus sot on Jasper,
    She never keered for Lou.

Well, people! Don't that beat you?
    Gone married Lou fo' spite;
The Lo'd have mussy on her!
    She's trapped herse'f for life.

Guess what ole Jeems been doin'?
    Can't guess to save my life;
Aint took a crazy notion
    To git another wife?

Fo' land-sakes! sister Harris,
    Ha! ha! ha! aint I beat?
That man's jest buyin' hosses
    Fo' crows an' dogs to eat.

Now, you know well as I do,
    He loses ev'ry one:
They're half dead when he gets them;
    I 'spect he thinks it's fun.

'Twus jest a week last Tuesday,
    Abe made me break my side,
Telling how the marshal fined him,
    For half bur'ing one that died.

I hearn 'bout sister Curtley?
    Why sistah Harris, no!
Fell down and broke her ankle?
    Good Lo'd! You don't say so?

Fell down them ole back do' steps!
    She told me they wus broke;
Ole Smith put off the fixing:
    I'd make that white man smoke!

I must git 'round and see her;
    Hope God will bring her through;
We must pray for her, Mandy,
    And see whut we can do.

We must not shirk our duty,
    And linger in the lurch,
But help, in tribulations,
    A sistah in the church.

You say you're feeling poorly?
    Then course you couldn't go;
Yes, Sistah Riley told me,
    That you wus feeling slow.

Now hush your 'pologizing!
    I know your heart is true;
Whut sistah did more shouting
    Last 'vival time than you?

You wa'n't out to meeting,
    When they 'churched' Riah Brown?
You'd broke your sides a-laughing,
    How Elder called him down.

The Elder riz and asked him,
    To take a seat in front;
So, up the aisle he shuffled,
    And sot down, with a grunt.

Then, spoke up Elder Mitchell,
    "Now, whut have you to say?
You know the charge against you,
    For the evil of your way.

"You've walked the way of sinnahs,
    Used church funds for your gain,
And when 'cused by Deacon Riley,
    Took the name of God, in vain."

Ef evah in your lifetime
    You've seen a good whooped hound,
With head and tail a-dragging,
    You then saw Riah Brown.

"And therefore," said the elder,
    His voice wus loud and stout,
"We want no wolves among us;
    I move to turn you out."

Poor sistah Brown wus crying,
    Riah wus sniffling too;
Yet seemed no sad occasion,
    Jest spite of all I'd do.

I know 'twa'n't like no [christian],
    The feeling that I had,
For ev'ry where around me,
    The sistahs looked so sad.

But 'pon my word, Amanda,
    Since my eyes first saw light,
I never felt more tickled,
    Than I did Tuesday night.

Then Riah says a sniffin',
    "I did do whut you say,
But bred'ren 'twas ole Satan,
    That coaxed me from the way."

You could a hearn a pin drop,
    When he commenced to say,—
"I'm but a umble critter;—"
    Laws, listen! Is that May?

Laws, honey! here's the child'en,
    School caint be out so soon;
Ef ever time went flyin',
    It did this afternoon.

That's right, I didn't finish,
    Well, I wus most nigh through,
You'll hear the rest tomorrow?
    I don't keer ef you do.

All right, tomorrow, Mandy,
    I'm mighty gled you come;
Now, don't fret 'bout them child'en,
    You'll find them safe at home.

And say, oh sistah Harris!
    Tomorrow, when you come,
Please tell old Mr. Bailey
    To send Abe's hatchet home.

The Muse's Favor

Oh Muse! I crave a favor,
    Grant but this one unto me;
Thou hast always been indulgent,
    So I boldly come to thee.

For oft I list thy singing,
    And the accents, sweet and clear,
Like the rhythmic flow of waters,
    Falls on my ecstatic ear.

But of Caucasia's daughters,
    So oft I've heard thy lay,
That the music, too familiar,
    Falls in sheer monotony.

And now, oh Muse exalted!
    Exchange this old song staid,
For an equally deserving:—
    The oft slighted, Afric maid.

The muse, with smiles, consenting,
    Runs her hand the strings along,
And the harp, as bound by duty,
    Rings out with the tardy song.

The Song
Oh, foully slighted Ethiope maid!
With patience, bearing rude upbraid,
With sweet, refined, retiring grace,
And sunshine lingering in thy face,

With eyes bedewed and pityingly,
I sing of thee, I sing of thee.

Thy dark and misty curly hair,
In small, neat braids entwineth fair,
Like clusters of rich, shining jet,
All wrapt in mist, when sun is set;
Fair maid, I gaze admiringly,
And sing of thee, and sing of thee.

Thy smooth and silky, dusky skin,
Thine eyes of sloe, thy dimple chin,
That pure and simple heart of thine,
'Tis these that make thee half divine;
Oh maid! I gaze admiringly,
And sing of thee, and sing of thee.

Oh modest maid, with beauty rare.
Whoe'er hath praised thy lithe form, fair?
Thy tender mien, thy fairy tread,
Thy winsome face and queenly head?
Naught of thy due in verse I see,
All pityingly I sing of thee.

Who's dared to laud thee 'fore the world,
And face the stigma of a churl?
Or brook the fiery, deep disdain,
Their portion, who defend thy name?
Oh maiden, wronged so cowardly,
I boldly, loudly sing of thee.

Who've stood the test of chastity,
Through slav'ry's blasting tyranny,
And kept the while their virtuous grace,

To instill in a trampled race?
Fair maid, thy equal few may see;
Thrice honored I to sing of thee.

Let cowards fear thy name to praise,
Let scoffers seek thee but to raze;
Despite their foul, ignoble jeers,
A worthy model thou appear,
Enrobed in love and purity;
Oh, who dare blush to sing of thee?

And now, oh maid, forgive, I pray,
The tardiness of my poor lay;
The weight of wrongs unto thee done
Did [paralyze] My falt'ring tongue;
'Twas my mute, innate sympathy,
That [stayed] this song I sing of thee.

The Favorite Slave's Story

Well, son, de story of my life
    Is long, and full of shade;
And yet, the bright spots, here and tha,
    A heap of comforts made.

When fust my eyes beheld de light,
    'Twas on a Chris'mus day,
Twelve miles fum Richmond "on a fa'm,"
    As you young upsta'ts say.

We said "plantation" in de South,
    We black- and white-folks too;
We wa'n't a changin' ev'ry day,
    Like all you young folks do.

My mother cooked de white-folks' grub,
    Dat's all she had to do.
Ole Miss, she spilte her half to death,
    And spilte her young ones, too.

Fah, well I mind me, in dem days,
    How I and Sue and Pete
Would roll around Miss Nancy's cheer,
    And play about her feet.

Miss Nancy,—I kin hear her yet—
    "You Petah, Sue, an' Si!
I'll make yo' maustah whoop you sho!"
    (Wid laughtah in her eye.)

Ole mause, he'd whoop us soon as not;
    But, when Miss Nancy saw,
She'd run out, wid dat look, an' say,
    "I wouldn't whoop him, Pa."

One day,—I nevah kin fahgit,
    Ole Miss wus sick in bed;
Ole Mause, he ripped, an' cussed, an' to',
    An' made himself a dread.

Somehow, I can't tell how it wus,
    He slapped my sistah Sue,
And mammy, coase she took it up,
    Den dah wus heap to do.

Pete lit right in wid tooth and claw,
    And so did little sis,
Fah me, I had anothah plan,
    I flew upstairs fah Miss.

I met Miss Nancy on de stairs,
    Wrapped in a great big shawl,
An' comin' down de steps so fast,
    Jest seemed as ef she'd fall.

I tried to tell her "whut wus up,"
    She pushed me on befo',
Fah mammy's cries wus in her yeahs,
    An' she heard nothin' mo'.

She caught ole Mause, an' pulled him off;
    Her eyes dey fa'ly blazed;
Ole Mause commenced a silly grin,
    An' looked like he wus dazed.*

I'd nevah seed Miss Nancy mad,
    Good Lo'd! She fussed an' to'e;
She "raked ole Maustah o'er de coals,"
    Until he begged an' swo'.

She wouldn't 'low Maria whooped,
    She jest would leave de place,
An' take 'way ev'ry slave she brought!
    She jest r'ared in his face.

She wouldn't 'low Maria whooped,
    Jest leave her young ones be!
They nevah sassed her when she spoke,
    It wasn't dem, 'twas he!

He tried to coax her back to bed,
    But, Lo'd! She wouldn't go:
Whut time had she to stay upstairs,
    When he would take on so?

An' Mammy, she wus cryin' loud;
    (De whoopin' wus her fus,)
An', whut wid little sistah Sue,
    It made Miss Nancy wus.

She'd fuss all 'round about Ole Mause,
    Jest like a spunky hen;
She'd pat my mothah on de back,
    An' den begin' again.

Well son, she p'intly made things wa'm,
    Fah Ole Mause whined an' swo';
No mattah how we all took on,
    He'd whoop none uv us mo'.

"Maria, take yo' Miss upstairs!"
  He'd wring his hands an' say;
Miss Nancy'd stamp her foot an' scream,
  She'd stay right tha' all day.

Well, when she'd fussed plum out uv bref,
  To add to his ala'ms,
She jest "keeled" ovah in a faint,
  An' fell into his a'ms.

Well, son, tha wus anothah stir;
  We young ones thought her dead;
Ole Mause, I b'lieve, he thought so too,
  Fah he plum lost his head.

Ole Miss wus sick fah quite a spell,
  An' mad right thue it all;
Fah when ole Mause cumed grinnin' roun',
  She'd turn an' face de wall.

So things went on, until one day,
  He axed her how she felt,
She reached out wid her ole time smile,
  So he cumed tha an' knelt.

Dey made it up, right dah an' den,
  An' as de day was fa',
He took her up into his a'ms,
  An' brung her down de sta'.

An' aftah dat, I tell you, son,
  Ole Mause, he let us be,
An' doe he slashed de othah slaves,
  Pete, Sue, an' me went free.

An' so de time went spinnin' on,
    Wid not a keer nor plan;
I didn't know whut trouble wus,
    Till I wus nigh a man.

Ole Fairfax owned my fathah, son,
    Dey lived across de creek.
De white-folks al'ays let him come,
    Three nights in ev'ry week.

Of coase he had his Sundays, too,
    Great days dey use' to be,
Fah all de blessed day he'd have
    We young ones 'bout his knee.

Or else, he'd take us all to church,
    All breshed up neat an' new,
Wid Mammy hanging to his arm,
    An' leading little Sue.

An' Mammy's eyes 'ud be so bright,
    When she had Pappy near;
She'd laugh an' giggle like a gal,
    But tryin' times drawed near.

Ole Mause an' Fairfax wus fast friends;
    A pa' uv roscals dey;
In gamblin', cheatin', an' de like,
    Dey bofe had heap to say.

So bofe got mixed up in a scrape
    Wid Richmond's bank, an' den,
Dey bofe sold ev'ry slave dey had,
    To keep out uv de pen.

I tell you son de good white-folks
    Wus good in time uv ease;
But soon as hawd times cummed tha' way,
    Dey'd change "quick as you please."

Soon as Miss Nancy seed de trap
    Ole Mause had done walked in,
She changed right dah, an who but she!
    A-helpin' him to sin.

Dey talked an' planned togethah, long;
    An', as de days flew by,
Miss Nancy changed an' got so cross
    Dat Mammy use' to cry.

One mawnin', jest to pick a fuss,
    She said she missed a pie;
When Mammy said dey all wus tha,
    She said, she told a lie:

Dat pie wus in her cabin, hid;
    She wus a vixen, bold;
An' ef she didn't bring it back,
    She'd have her whooped an' sold.

Well, son, you see dat wus her scheme,
    To sell her, wid de rest;
An' aftah dat, she made it plain,
    To all uv us, I 'fess.

An' so, at last, de day rolled 'round,
    When all, exceptin' I,
Wus put upon de block an' sold,
    To any one who'd buy.

Oh, son! You don't know whut it is,
    To see yo' loved ones sold,
An' hear de groans, an' see de tears,
    Uv young, as well as ole.

An' see dem white men bus'lin' 'roun',
    A-feelin' uv yo' a'm,
An' havin' you to run an' skip,
    An' caper till you's wa'm.

An' all de while, wid questions, keen,
    An' wid a [watchful] eye,
Not keerin' how yo' h'a't might ache,
    Jest so you's strong an' spry.

Po' Mammy! How kin I fahgit,
    Her pa'tin' from us all?
Dat pa'tin', son, will 'bide wid me,
    Until de Lo'd will call!

'Way down de rivah, she wus sold,
    Alone, wid no kin nigh;
Her tendah h'a't broke 'fo' she left,
    I know she's long on High.

An' Pappy, Pete, an' little Sue
    Wus sent their dif'rent ways,
An' not one has my eyes beheld,
    Since dem sad, pa'tin' days.

Oh son, you don't know how I felt,
    When all dat stir wus past!
Sometimes I'd git to grievin' so,
    I thought I couldn't last.

De empty cabins all aroun',
   De stables empty, too,
Miss Nancy cryin' day an' night,
   Ole Mause a-lookin' blue.

I tell you son, dem [tryin' days]
   Aw burnt into my soul:
I feel de pain, I see it all,
   Same as dem days uv old.

Ah well! De sun will sometimes shine,
   E'en in a po' slave's life;
De Lo'd healed up my broken h'a't,
   By sendin' me a wife.

Miss Nancy wus as good to her,
   An' spilte her jest as bad
As she did mammy long befo',
   Sometimes it made me sad.

Ole Mause had prospered, bought mo' slaves,
   Ole Miss wus sweet an' kind;
My little ones an' Charlotte, dear,
   Had pushed my grief behind.

I al'ays wus Miss Nancy's pet,
   She made it very plain;
An' I must say, in all my grief,
   She tried to ease my pain.

An' now dat I wus gay once mo',
   An' happy as could be,
She petted Charlotte an' my chaps,
   An' seemed as pleased as me.

So time sped on widout a keer,
    Save whut had long since past,
Till Ole Mause's health begin to fail,
    An' son, he went down fast.

He took on scan'lous in dem days,
    When he saw death wus nigh;
He cussed an' to' from mawn till night;
    It made Miss Nancy cry.

He nevah had been conquered, son,
    By any living thing,
So, when grim Death lay hold uv him,
    He fit ha'd 'gainst de sting.

But, son, at last he'd found his match,
    Fah 'spite uv all his rage,
Ole Satan flung his fi'ry hook,
    An' pulled him in his cage.

You nevah seed a sinnah die,
    So son you jest don't know;
You could 've heard Ole Maustah cuss
    Fuh half a mile or mo'.

He axed me fuh a class uv gin,
    He jest wus crazy med;
He bit de rim from off de glass,
    An' spit it on de bed.

An' den he yelled, "Look at him, Si!
    Drive that black dog away!
He's snapping at my throat, you see,
    Ketch hold his chain, I say!"

He would've sprung plum out de bed,
    Had I not held him in;
Den, wid a long an' doleful yell,
    He died in all his sin.

De wah, dat had been grumblin' roun',
    Broke full about dis time;
De slaves begun a-walkin' off,
    To suit their own free mind.

Ole Miss wus cryin' day an' night,
    An' beggin' me to stay,
While Charlotte urged me, on de sly,
    To go North, fah away.

I looked into her pleadin' eyes,
    So helpless, trustin' me,
An' den, upon my little chaps,
    An' manhood said, "Be free!"

Ole Missus cumed down to de gate;
    To bid fahwell, she tried,
But she jest held fast bofe our hands,
    An' cried, an' cried, an' cried.

An' so we cumed up to dis state,
    An' worked on, bes' we could,
A-trustin' al'ays in de Lo'd,
    An' tryin' to be good.

We raised our chaps, dey all done well,
    An' now have settled down,
Exceptin' Jane, our baby gal,
    Who you aw co'ting now.

You say you want her fah yo' wife?
    I know, uv co'se you do;
I give consent, fah son you see,
    I al'ays did like you.

Dat lifts a burden from my mind;
    You're young, an' good, an' true;
We've lived to see our othahs thrive,
    We want Jane settled, too.

Take good keer uv our baby, son,
    A tendah child she be,
Why, look! Here she an' Charlotte comes;
    She's told her Ma, you see.

The Interrupted Reproof

Zella Wheeler! did I evah?
    Playing with yo' ole dolls; Well!
Great, big gal, here, tall as mammy,
    Big a baby as Estelle!

I'll tell daddy, Miss, this eb'nin',
    And he'll pleg yo' life out sho';
Great big gal, with beaux a-comin',
    Crawlin' 'round heah on the flo'!

Sunday noon, gwine tell the Elder;
    Sunday night, I'm gwine tell Ed;
Needn't come heah tryin' to hug me!
    You caint coax it out my head.

Yo' ole mammy's not gwine keep it,
    Ed's gwine 'o hear it sho's you bo'n;
Shame on you! An' Ed a co'ting.
    Playing dolls heah all the mo'n.

Them's yo' dolls! Think I don't know them,
    When I bought them all myse'f?
Needn't try, caint fool yo' mammy.
    Them's Estelle's tha on the shef.

Gwine tell Ed, and gwine tell daddy—
    What's that noise! Who's that out tha'?
Give me them dolls, Lawd, here's Eddie!
    Mussy sakes! Go bresh yo' ha'.

Freedom at McNealy's

All around old Chattanooga,
    War had left his wasteful trace;
And the rebels, quelled and baffled,
    Freed reluctantly their slaves.

On his spacious, cool veranda—
    Stood McNealy, gaunt and tall,
With bowed head, and long arms folded,
    Pondering on his blacks, enthralled.

Years, and years, he'd been their master,
    Harsh and stern his reign had been;
Many an undeserving lashing
    He had rudely given them.

All his life he'd been a despot,
    Ruling all with iron hand;
Never till this deadly conflict
    Had he e'er brooked one command.

But his lately rich plantation,
    Sacked by Union men he see;
And the bitter dregs stand waiting:
    He must set his bondmen free.

From their work, they come together,
    At their master's last command,
And at length, well-nigh two hundred,
    'Fore the large veranda stand.

Oh! that motley crowd before him,
    Speaks the wrong one man has done;
For his constant, dire oppression
    Can be seen on every one.

Men of middle age all palsied,
    By hard work and sorrow's pain,
Blighted youths and orphaned infants,
    All had felt his cruel reign.

There were women fair, who knew him
    To be [more of] brute than man;
There were children clinging to them,
    Through whose veins his own blood ran.

Widowed hearts in swarthy bosoms
    Ever bled in patient pain,
O'er their loved ones, sold before them,
    To increase McNealy's gain.

All of this preys on McNealy,
    As before his slaves he stands;
And his low'ring, dogged expression
    Speaks the power that's left his hands.

And, with quivering voice and husky,
    Tells he that each one is free,
Tells them of his heavy losses,
    Meanly seeking sympathy.

And the soft hearts of his vassals
    Melt, as only Ethiopes' can,
As with brimming eyes and kind words,
    Each one grasps his tyrant's hand.

One by one, they've all departed,
    Man and woman, boy and girl,
Void of learning, inexperienced,
    Launched upon the crafty world.

But one cabin is not empty:
    Two old souls are kneeling there;
In the throes of desolation,
    They have sought their Lord in prayer.

They have never tasted freedom,
    And their youthful hopes are fled;
Now, the freedom they are seeking
    Is with Jesus, and the dead.

Poor aunt Jude and uncle Simon!
    Freedom brings to them no cheer;
They have served McNealy's fam'ly,
    For three-score or more of years.

Steep and rough, the road the've traveled,
    Many were their heart felt groans,
Yet they cleave unto their tyrant,
    For his lash is all they've known.

Like a bird of long confinement
    Cleaves unto his open cage,
These two wretched slaves, benighted,
    Clave to bondage, in their age.

And they sought McNealy humbly,
    With their hearts filled to the brim;
Told him, all their days remaining,
    They would gladly give to him.

And McNealy, pleased and flattered,
    With no feeling of remorse,
Takes them back into his service,
    As you would a faithful horse.

Adown the Heights of Ages

Adown the heights of Ages,
    Where mist oft dims the view,
Where blinding chaos rages,
    Whilst sweet peace mingles, too,
A caravan e'er moves along,
A fast increasing, fitful throng,*
    To whom we've said adieu.*

Oft, through the mist, seclusive,
    Familiar forms appear;
And from their realm, exclusive,
    Their joys and griefs we hear;
A bright ray oft lights up the mist,
And flash us back a loving kiss,
    Or counsel we hold dear.

And often, in the young night,
    When memories beguile,
We drift behind the foot-lights,
    And play with them awhile;
'Tis then we press that hand, again,
And hear that voice, that thrills to pain,
    And drink again that smile.

Then stroll we through the wildwood,
    Down to the meadow brook,
And with the joy of childhood,
    We ply our fishing hook;
Or, in the country school, once more,
We take our places, "on the floor,"
    Intent with slate and book.

Or else, with joy and laughter,
    We join the social feast,
Which brings the smile long after
    The hour of mirth has ceased;
We catch those love-lit eyes, as bright
As e'er they shone that long fled night,
    And feel our glad heart leap.

And so we drift, forgetful
    Of all except the past,
'Til with a start, regretful,
    We find ourselves, at last;
The drama fades before our eye;
We yield our loved ones, with a sigh,
    Back, to relentless past.

Thus down the heights of Ages,
    A mere yote in the throng,
All that our life engages,
    Moves speedily along;
Small, small, indeed, the part we play,
The hour glass wastes the sand away,
    Ere half is sung, Life's song.

After the Quarrel

Lindie, chile, fo' Lawd sake, tell me
    Whut's come ovah you an' Link?
'Mos' fo' weeks since he's called on you,
    Time he's comin' back, I think.

'Tain't no use to cry now, Honey.
    Mussy! how de chile takes on!
Mammy knows well how yo' h'a't aches,
    Done felt all, chile, fo' you's bo'n.

Felt dat, when yo' Pa wus co'tin';
    Lawd! I've felt it day on day!
Honey, Sugah, hesh yo' cryin'!
    Can't make out a word you say.

Oh, I see! Link's done got jealous!
    Didn't I say it wa'n't so sma't,
Prancin' 'round wid Elex Johnson,
    When [you] know, Link's got yo' h'a't.

I go tell him dat you love him?
    Lindie, ain't you goin' med?
Tink yo' Mammy'd stoop to dat trick,
    Tink I'd frow you at his head?

Wha's de dignity I taught you,
    While you growed up by my side?
Didn't mean it? Dat sound bettah,
    Knowed you had Virginia pride.

Honey, chile, yo' Ma feels fo' you,
    Hesh yo' cryin', brace up prim.
Don't you know dat Link is grievin'
    Much fo' you as you fo' him?

Yes indeed! Link's not fo'got you,
    He'll quit poutin' by an' by.
Den he'll love you mo'en evah,
    'Twas dat way wid Pa an' I.

Dah, you laugh; dat's bettah, Honey.
    But now mind, when Link comes back,
You leave Elex to Lize Posten,
    An' jest trot on yo' own track.

Song of the Moon

Oh, a hidden power is in my breast,
    A power that none can fathom;
I call the tides from seas of rest,
They rise, they fall, at my behest;
And many a tardy fisher's boat
I've torn apart and set afloat,
    From out their raging chasm.

For I'm an enchantress, old and grave;
    Concealed I rule the weather;
Oft set I the lover's heart ablaze,
With hidden power of my fulgent rays,
Or seek I the souls of dying men,
And call the sea-tides from the fen,
    And drift them out together.

I call the rain from the mountain's peak,
    And sound the mighty thunder;
When I wax and wane from week to week,
The heavens stir, while vain men seek
To solve the myst'ries that I hold,
But a bounded portion I unfold,
    So nations pass and wonder.

Yea, my hidden strength no man may know,
    Nor myst'ries be expounded;
I'll cause the tidal waves to flow,
And I shall wane, and larger grow,
Yet while man rack his shallow brain,
The secrets with me still remain.
    He seeks in vain, confounded.

Insulted

My Mamma is a mean old sing,
    An' toss as she tan be;
I'm doeing to pack my doll trunt,
    An' doe to G'an'ma Lee.

My Mamma baked a dinger tate,
    Den panked me shameful hard,
Dust 'tause I stuck my finder in,
    An' filled de holes wiz lard.

If I was down to G'an'ma Lee,
    She'd say, "Ionie, shame!"
And fen I 'ud tommence to ky,
    She'd call me pitty names.

But Mamma, fus, she slapped my ear,
    Den jerked me fum de chair,
And panked and flung me on de lounge,
    An' said, "You dus' lay dere!"

I'm doein' to tell my Papa, too,
    Fen he tum home tonight,
He'll take me back to g'an'ma,
    An' out of Mamma's sight.

An' fen she det so lonesome,
    Like she did las' week, an' kied,
I won't yun out an' tiss her,
    I'm doeing 'way, an' hide.

Soft Black Eyes

Soft black eyes, all pensive, tender,
    Changeful as a shifting ray;
Now, in sympathy they linger,
    Now, in mirth, they flash away.
    Orbs of midnight, like a dart,
    Doth thou pierce my aching heart!

Soft black eyes, half coy, half artless,
    Half in earnest, half in jest,
Well I know thou art not heartless,
    Yet thy tricks doth pain my breast.
    Orbs of night, gaze a caress,
    Thou, alone, my life canst bless!

Soft black eyes, so sweet and soothing,
    Knowest thou from day to day,
My sad life in sighs I'm losing,
    Sighing heart and soul away?
    Let my plight, those stars molest!
    Sympathy will give me rest.

Raphael

Behold young Raphael coming back;
    How long the time doth seem,
Since last he parted from the side
    Of her, his sweetest dream.

And yet a fortnight scarce hath past,
    Since last he left her side,
And saw these soft eyes fill with tears,
    His love, his joy, his pride.

And now he's coming back again,
    A husband's place to hold;
He seeks communion with himself,
    And saunters 'cross the wold.

With polished rifle on his arm,
    And hunting coat of gray,
His Pilot trotting at his heel,
    With joy he winds his way.

Though Raphael is a marksman fair,
    Of hunting over fond,
Ere yet, he lifteth not his gun,
    To bring the good game down.

But now doth rouse he from his dream,
    And cocks his trusty gun;
For he hath reached the willowed dell,
    Where deer is wont to run.

The day is calm, soft breezes blow,
    And all is still as dawn;
Upon the lake, among the rush,
    Are floating flocks of swan.

Then saith young Raphael, as he gaze
    On rush and willows 'round,
"The truant deer hath sought the cliffs,
    And naught but swan I've found.

"I'll choose the whitest of the flock."
    Thus did young Raphael speak:
"As symbol of the pure young heart
    Of her, whose hand I seek."

And so, adown the dell he peers,
    And through the rush he sees
A mass of downy whiteness there,
    Half hidden by the leaves.

He lifts his gun, he takes good aim,
    And forward Pilot start:
Triumphantly he lowers his piece;
    He knows he's hit the mark.

Oh luckless youth, retrace thy steps!
    The sight that waits thine eyes
Will turn thy ebon locks to snow,
    And waste thy life with sighs.

Oh deadly bullet, why so true?
    What havoc thou hast wrought,
To turn into the deepest grief
    Young Raphael's noblest thought!

For there, half hidden by the rush,
    Doth lie a heap like snow;
Poor Pilot whines and licks the face
    Of one full well he know.

And now, young Raphael's coming up;
    He puts the rush aside,
And there upon the sward beholds
    His game—his own loved bride.

One look reveals his waiting love,
    All clad in snowy white,
Her angel face, her bosom red—
    He groans—and all is night.

Oh young, heart-broken, weary youth!
    God chasteneth whom he love;
Thy thoughts were ever with thy bride;
    They never soared above.

But since the one thou lovest so well
    Hast flown to realms of rest,
Thy whole soul turneth to thy God,
    And yearneth for the blest.

And when thy keenest grief is past,
    And hushed thy deepest sighs,
Thou'lt deem her but an angel sent,
    To lure thee to the skies.

A Domestic Storm

I'm goin' to whoop you, Sammy Taylor,
    Done gone eat nigh half my pie!
"Please Ma, honest, no I never."
    Hesh dat tellin' me dat lie!

Here's de prints uv dirty fingahs,
    As you tilted up de lid;
Here, you smeared de plate wid grape juice;
    "No'm, I didn't." Yes, you did!

Ma'ch yourse'f right in dis kitchen!
    "Please, I didn't steal it Mum.
See, I've been out hunting bird eggs,
    Jest got back afore you come."

Hunting bird eggs! didn't I tell you
    Dat 'twas wrong to pester birds?
Thought I told you to mind Viney,
    Don't you say another word!

Den you didn't steal de grape-pie,
    Do some meanness doe you would;
Wonder, den, if Viney eat it?
    Ef she did, I'll whoop her good.

Viney!—"Ma'am!"—Ma'ch in dis kitchen;
    'Taint no use fo' you to cry;
I can see as plain as daylight,
    Dat 'twus you dat eat de pie.

Eat dat pie Miss Julie sent me,
 When Jim cya'ed de washin' home!
You knowed dat you'd got yo' po'tion,
 Ef you went an' left it 'lone.

Ef you wont hear to Miss Vi'let,
 Whut she teach in Sunday School,
Den I'll try anothah method,
 I will whoop you to de rule.

Where's my switch? Jest ti'ed uv foolin';
 Ought to done dis long befo'!
"O-o-o! Please Ma dont whoop no harder!
 Honest! I won't steal no mo'!"

Sit right down da' in dat cornah;
 Stop dat sniffin'! wipe dat nose!
Ef I'd set, and let you do it,
 Next you'd eat de house I s'pose.

An' you's been out huntin' bird eggs,
 'Spite uv all I said to you,
When I told you to mind Viney!
 Dah, now! Dah! "Please, Mammie, oo-o-o!

"I won't never steal no bird eggs,
 Please quit whoopin' Mammie, do!
I'll mind Viney good the next time!"
 Guess you will, you rascal, you.

A Little Wren

A wren dropped down on my window sill,
    And his little feet was hid in the snow;
Yet he tossed me a saucy glance, as to say,
    I'm happy out here where the ice wind blow,
And life seems bright and cheerful as May;
    And you inside, in your soft armchair,
        Seems half in content and half in [despair].

And coyly he frisked about in the snow,
    And the white flakes flew from his dainty feet,
And airily lifting his little right wing,
    With latest wren etiquette me did he greet,
Then dashed he away, with a merry swing;
And I thought as he scurried away from my sight,
Contentment is his who reads it aright.

He was without and I was within;
    Yet he had the sunshine, I had the shade;
With life as it was, he e'er could rejoice,
    While I must be pampered, and comforts be made,
Ere I my jubilant joys could voice;
And I thought as I mused on the failings of man,
Which does God deems wisest, the sage or the wren?

In the Valley

Oh God! my heart is thine,
    Content, am I, in Thee;
Thy chast'ning rod but proves
    That Thou abides with me.

I know Thou leadeth on,
    But oh, the way is drear;
Naught, but the click of thorns,
    Is sounding in my ear.

I cry, "Thy will be done!"
    My heart is with the cry,
Yet comes not light, nor peace,
    To soothe my tear-dim eye.

My heart craves earthly things;
    I feel its nature's claim;
Since Thou didst give me life,
    Canst I discard an aim?

The hot blood stirs my brain,
    And sweet dreams to me flock;
Alas! I see them wrecked
    Upon Ambition's rock.

Oh Christ! Come down to earth,
    An elder brother, be;
And pilot Thou, my barque,
    Which drifts capriciously.

Oh wrench me from the toils
    Of this entangled mesh!
My spirit strives for Thee,
      Despite the erring flesh.

Address to Ethiopia

Oh, ill-starred Ethiopian—
    My weak and trampled race!
With fathomless emotion,
    Thy dismal path I trace.

Thy bright and stalwart, swarthy sons,
    Thy meek-eyed daughters, fair,
I trace through centuries bygone
    Of misery and despair.

Thy fathers' fathers, long were taught,
    Nay, forced by tyrants, bold,
To worship at a mortal shrine,
    With humble heart and soul.

So long hath slav'ry's blasting hand
    O'er thee its power swayed,
That now, though freedom sweet is thine,
    I see thee cowed and dazed.

The sin is at thy tyrant's door;
    The curse is at thine own;
And e'er will rest upon thy head,
    Till thou wilt tear it down.

Oh! rouse thy slumb'ring manhood, strong!
    A foothold boldly earn;
And scorn thy brothers' patronage,
    When he's thy fellow-worm.

Tear down those idols thou hast built,
    In weakness, to the proud!
Knowest thou that in thy blindness, deep,
    Thou desecrate thy God?

Oh! rise in union great and strong!
    Hold each black brother dear,
And form a nation of thine own,
    Despite thy tyrant's jeers!

We need not reek in blood and groans,
    This is a war within;
We need but conquer cow'ring self,
    And rise a man, with men.

What though our number may be few?
    Hath not the Jews long stood,
In unions strong, 'mid myriads
    Of foes who craved their blood?

Then, rise, oh fainting Ethiopes!
    And gather up thy strength;
For, by repeated efforts, strong,
    Thou'lt gain thy ground at length.

The same God hast created thee,
    Who did thy fairer brother;
Thinkst thou, that in His justice, great,
    He'd prize one 'bove the other?

Autumn

List to the sad wind, drearily moaning,
    Moaning the fate of the choicest and best;
Seest those red leaves descending in torrents?
    'Tis blood drops of warriors sinking to rest.
Many a volley they've turned in their glory,
Now, lack-a-day! They perish, all gory.

Ever they conquered and victory boasted,
    O'er storm and o'er drought and vollies of rain,
Showing more strength when battle was over,
    And bearing off laurels again and again.
Flushed with success, did they go forth rejoicing.
Now their ill-fate, the sad wind is voicing.

Fiercely the frost-king urged on his subjects,
    Spreading destruction o'er hillside and fen!
Yet bravely they fought, not one e'er despairing,
    Till gushing with life-blood, they fell down like men.
Now the pathos of death the last scene is lending,
Who'd have believe such a fate was impending?

Lines to Emma

Oh, could I but sing as the minstrels of old!
    Whose beautiful love songs ring still in our ear!
    In accents so musical, rhythmical, clear,
    Now soaring majestical, now hov'ring near,
With passionate tenderness, shy and yet bold,
    That enamored his lady-love, ruffled her breast,
    And drew her frail form to his bosom, for rest!

Oh, could I, my sweetheart charm thus to my breast,
    Methink overflowing my cup would then be;
    To gaze to the depth of those eyes' liquid sea,
    And cause them to waver and droop before me,
And to feel my glad heart throb wild with the zest,
    While tenderly holding her in my embrace,
    And feasting my eyes on her fair, angel face.

But alas I am luckless, dear Emma the best,
    And sternly hath Cupid dealt fate unto me;
    To stir my love passion, and yet let me see
    A maiden that yearneth another's to be,
And yearns not in vain to be queen of his breast,
    For my bosom too often has felt that keen dart
    To be wrong in sounding a brother's sore heart.

Uncle Jimmie's Yarn

Did I evah tell you, Sonny,
    Well, a-he! he! he!
  De trick I played in Dixie,*
    'Way back in 'sixty-three?
I wus wild an' full uv mischief,
    An' reckless ez could be,
In dem rough ole days in Natchez,
    'Way back in 'sixty-three.

I wus out a-for'gin', Sonny,
    Well, a he! he! he!
  Out a-doin' debbilment,
    Big man sah, who but me?
Had a smackin' big hoss-pistol,
    'Long 'bout dis size, confound!
Jest to wa'm dem rebels' jackets,
    An' make dem jump around.

It wus early Sunday mawnin',
    Well, a-he! he! he!
  When all de boys wus restin',
    'Cept sma'ties, jest like me.
I, astride my coal black filly,
    Cumed a-lopin' up de hill,
Whar I halted an' sot lookin',
    Down Natchez, ca'm an' still.

I could see de great big buildin's,
    Well, a-he! he! he!
  A r'arin' up tha steeples,
    Dat seemed a sassin' me.

Den I pulled ole roa'in' [Betsy],
  An' aimed de cupelo,
Uv de co'thouse uv de rebels,
  An' let de triggah go.

I wus handy wid a pistol,
  Well a he! he! he!
 My han' wus true an' stiddy,*
  Fuh I wus young, you see.
So my fust shot [to'] a slab off,
  Nigh big ez dat ba'n doe;
Dat jest riled me wus dan evah,
  So, once mo' I let huh go.

Den de othah side, I leveled,
  Well, a-he! he! he!
 She jest to'e tings to pieces,
  Ez any eye could see.
So den, nuttin' but de centah pa't
  Uv dat fine cupelo
Wus a-standin' now fuh Natchez,
  De rest wus layin' low.

Den I loaded roa'in' Betsy,
  Well, a-he! he! he!
 An' cracked it on de centah,*
  An' Betsy bawled out, Dee!
De centah pa't jest crumbled down,
  Sho Sonny, yes sah ree!
So dat settled wid dat co't-house,
  'Way back in 'sixty-three.

Den I wheeled, an' spurred my filly,
    Well, a he! he! he!
  An' put off fuh de barracks,
    Ez fas' ez fas' could be.
I could heah de bullets whislin',
    About my very head,
Fuh I'd hit de rebel's bee-hive,
    An' dey answered me wid lead.

When [at last] I reached de barracks,
    Well, a-he! he! he!
  Do captain standin' 'kimbo,
    Wus fus man dat I see.
"Whut's you doin' to dem rebels?
    You vagabond," he sed.
"You raised mo' fuss an' smoke down dah,
    Dan evah could ole Ned."

Den de laugh his eyes 'gin twinklin',
    Well, a-he! he! he!
  An' so I bust out laughin',
    I seed dat I wus free.
"You'll git yo' fill uv fightin', sah,
    You roscil!" den says he,
And dat wound up de co't-house scrape,
    'Way back in 'sixty-three.

Oh, Whence Comes the Gladness?

Oh, whence comes the gladness?
The joy fraught with madness?
    The hopes and the fancies of childhood's bright
        day?
The weird exultation,
And rife animation,
    That sets all the heart strings
    A-chord with the May?

From whence comes the Wonder-Land?
Likewise the Fairy land?
    The halo encircling, the trifles of life?
The bright dream materialized?
The bear and wolf humanized?
    The bugbear, the [werewolf],
    And fair water sprite?

Then searched I with lightness,
The summer sun's brightness;
    There caught I a glimpse of this coveted mirth,
Then sought I the South Wind,
Among the rank clinging vine,
    And caught it once more,
    As it fled from the earth.

A Kindly Deed

A thought flashed 'cross a kindly mind,
    It grew into a deed;
A deed that stretched a helping hand,
    Unto a brother's need.

That brother, strengthened by the deed,
    In humble gratitude,
Passed on the blessing he received,
    To do another good.

And on it went, and years passed by,
    'Til, as the maxim run,
This deed, around its circuit, passed,
    Returned where it begun.

It found its owner sunken low,
    In heartache's bitter groan;
The thought, the deed of that far day,
    Proved but a friendly loan.

The Old Freedman

He sits in front of the bright, blazing grate,
    A poor old freedman, maimed and gray.
With worn hands folded, he sits and waits
    His Master's summons, from day to day.
His ebon brow is seamed deeply with care;
    His dim eyes, robbed of their scanty sight
By the dazzling red of the ember's glare,
    Sets him to dreaming as [though] 'twere night.

And his hard, early life comes, scene by scene,
    As acts appear on a play-house stage,
While he sits with a thoughtful smile, serene,
    And views the past, in a dreamy maze.
Yes, now he can smile as he thinks on those days,
    For the fire of youth has long fled his breast;
He has cast the burden of past care away,
    And humbly looks to his Master, for rest.

He hears the fierce screams of his mother, wild,
    Anguished and startling, and loud as of old,
While haplessly he, her remaining child,
    Is hurried "down the river," and sold.
And now comes the scene of that sugar farm,
    Where the lash and fever rules supreme,
Where the humid, sickly atmosphere, warm,
    Brings on a giddiness, e'en in his dream.

He is hoeing cane, with a stalwart pace,
    And with him, a girl, the joy of his life,
With her graceful figure and dark brown face,
    And her sunny smile—his own fair wife.

When e'er the overseer's back is turned,
    He lends a strong hand to her lagging row,
That her exacting task may be earned,
    To ward from her back, the brutal blow.

Despite the appalling crosses of life,
    He deems himself e'en a happy man,
Just to have her near and to call her "wife,"
    And to hurriedly press her little worn hand.
The third scene is on, and now he behold
    His Lucy coming with eyes filled with tears;
"Oh Ruben," she's crying, "why I'm to be sold!"
    The words fall like doom upon his shocked ears.

Again that dull giddiness rises within,
    His lower limbs weaken, he rests on his hoe;
He feels her embraces again and again,
    Then turns she, and back to the "big house" doth go.
Her fleeting form brings him back to himself;
    He drops his hoe, with a desperate groan;
He'll make the rude trader take back his foul pelf;
    He'll claim his wife, for she is his own.

Oh, futile struggle! he sees his fair love
    Borne off by the rude, evil trader, who spoils,
While he helplessly calls on his Father above,
    And is fiercely, brutally lashed for his toils.
Oh, let us pass over the dark days that came,
    And rev'rently screen this act of his life!
When the anguish of Rizpah, who mourned for her slain,
    Could not be compared with his grief o'er his wife.

And now, clears the smoke, that is black as the night;
    He stands firm a giant with Gettysburg's brave;
The death blows he deals, in the hand to hand fight,
    Serve vengeance to rebels who late held him slave.
And now, he is come to the calm years of peace,
    His restless wand'rings in search of his wife;
When despaired and discouraged, his wanderings cease,
    And he fills with religion, the void of his life.

And now the last scene, the triumphant, the grand!
    With dim sight renewed and infirmities fled,
Fair Lucy once more is pressing his hand,
    And Jesus is placing a crown on his head.
For there, in front of the bright, blazing grate,
    With a sad, kind smile, and expressionless eye,
At the end of the day, in the even, late,
    He had taken his flight, to his home on high.

The Old Year

Infirm and aged doth he sit,
    And ponder on the gilded past;
His brilliant eyes, alas, death-lit,
    Is like a spark, too bright to last.

And muses he on days now sped,
    When he, a youth, with staff and thong,
Pursued the waning year, that fled,
    And left him monarch brave and strong.

What happy days they seem to be,
    Now that they number with the past;
But hark! those distant shouts of glee!
    He cuts his musings with a gasp.

With bony hands he grasps his cape,
    And wraps it 'bout his trembling form;
Then turns, a humped, decrepit shape,
    And flees the coming of the morn.

And as his wasted form doth drift,
    All mist-like, through the frosty air,
Close in the rear, behold a rift,
    And through it comes the glad New Year.

SONGS FROM THE WAYSIDE

Clara Ann Thompson

Dedicated to My Brother and Sister,
Garland and Priscilla

To My Dead Brother

How silently the years have sped away,
    Drifting me off from childhood's sunny time,
Since angels bore thy pure white soul away,
    On swift bright wings, to realms of fairer day,
And purer clime.

And still my heart, dear brother, yearns for thee;
    When friends seem cold, and life and earth so drear,
Thou wert my hero, ever true to me;
Though other brothers loved I tenderly,
    Thou wert most dear.

Ofttimes when death seems cold and grim to me,
I cling to earth, with all its wasting care,
    I think: That Messenger once came to thee;
And then I dare to brave eternity,
    For thou art there.

And when, at last, the toil of life all o'er,
    I stand by Jordan's surging, swelling tide,
Methinks our Lord will send thee to the shore,
    To guide thy falt'ring, timid sister o'er
        To heaven's side.

Uncle Rube's Defense

Whut do I keer ef de white-folks do 'buse us!
    I'm go'n to stand fuh de cullud race;
Whut do I keer ef de roscals do 'cuse us
    All, when dere's only one man in disgrace?

White-folks a-thievin' and rahin' an' kickin',
    Uddah white-folks ez still ez a mouse;
Aftahwhile, somebody steals a few chickens,
    Den, dey wan' to search old Deacon Jones' house.

Habn't proved yet dat a cullud man took dem;
    "Coons gen'ly steal de chickens," dey say,
Runnin' 'roun' here a-peepin' and a-lookin',
    Givin' de re'l thief a chance to git away.

Ev'ry low trick dat de black man's a-doin'
    'Flects right back on de race, as a whole;
But de low co'se dat de white man's pursuin'
    Casts not a blot on his good brudder's soul.

Let de black man do somepin wuth mentionin',
    White-folks ez still and shy ez a fawn;
Let him do somepin dat's mean an' belittlin',
    Umph! den de whole race has got it an' gone.

I don't deny dat some blacks is a-tryin'
    Hawd to make de race 'pear like a cuss,
But do ez dey will,—you know I ain't lyin',
    Dere's white-folks a doin' de same er wuss.

Memorial Day

Go;—for 'tis Memorial morning—
    Go with hearts of peace and love;
Deck the graves of fallen soldiers;
    Go, your gratitude to prove.

Gather flow'rs and take them thither,
    Emblem of a nation's tears;
Grateful hearts cannot forget them,
    In the rush of passing years.

Strew the flow'rs above their couches;
    Let thy heart's affection blend
With the dewy buds and blossoms,
    That in fragrant showers descend.

Strew the flow'rs above the heroes,
    Slain for loving friends and thee;
Canst thou find a better off'ring,
    For those sons of liberty?

While the buds and blooms are falling,
    Earnest hearts are asking,—"Why?"—
In a tone, though low and gentle,
    Yet, as ardent as a cry.—

"Why must precious lives be given,
    That our country may be free?
Is there not a nobler pathway
    To the throne of liberty?

"Can we choose no nobler watch-word
    Than the ringing battle-cry,
Harbinger of strife and bloodshed;
    Must we sin, that sin may die?

"Long ago, to far Judea,
    Came the blessed Prince of Peace;
Shall we ever heed His teaching,
    That these wars and feuds may cease?"

Johnny's Pet Superstition

Teacher, Jimmie's toe is bleedin';
    Stumped it, comin' down the road;
I jest knowed that he would do it,
    'Cause he went an' killed a toad.

Teacher, you jest ought to see it;
    Oh, the blood's jest spurtin' out!
You won't ketch me killin' toad-frogs,
    When I see them hoppin' 'bout.

"Oh, now, Johnny, that's all nonsense!
    I told you sometime ago,
That the killing of a hop-toad
    Wouldn't make you hurt your toe;

"Who told you that silly story?"
    Grandma said that it is so;
She's much older than you, teacher,
    An' I guess she ought to know.

"Come, now, Johnny, don't be saucy";
    Teacher, grandma did say so,
An' she says: "You No'thern cullud,
    Don't b'lieve nothin' any mo'.

'Cause you say there ain't no speerits,
    'Tain't bad luck to kill a cat,
Dog a-howlin' ain't no death-sign."
    An' you've made me b'lieve all that.

But I jest can't b'lieve this, teacher,
    'Cause I'm 'fraid to—Don't you see?
Bet you wouldn't b'lieve it either,
    Ef you went barefoot, like me.

Hope

The saddest day will have an eve,
    The darkest night, a morn;
Think not, when clouds are thick and dark,
    Thy way is too forlorn.

For, ev'ry cloud that e'er did rise
    To shade thy life's bright way,
And ev'ry restless night of pain,
    And ev'ry weary day,

Will bring thee gifts thou'lt value more,
    Because they cost so dear;
The soul that faints not in the storm
    Emerges bright and clear.

The Dying Year

The snow is weaving a soft, white shroud,
    For the dying year, today;
The wind is chanting a solemn dirge,
    The sky is dull and gray.

All earth is mourning for the year,
    And, with an echo of pain,
Our hearts beat time to the sad wind's song,
    As the Old Year ends his reign.

Ah, dying year! thy reign was brief,
    A fitful, fleeting breath;
Erewhile, rejoiced we at thy birth,
    And now, we mourn thy death.

And yet, dear, dying, fleeting year,
    Why should we mourn for thee?
All earth will follow thee, erelong,
    Into eternity.

His Answer

He prayed for patience; Care and Sorrow came,
    And dwelt with him, grim and unwelcome guests;
He felt their galling presence night and day;
And wondered if the Lord had heard him pray,
    And why his life was filled with weariness.

He prayed again; and now he prayed for light;
    The darkness parted, and the light shone in;
And lo! he saw the answer to his prayer—
His heart had learned, through weariness and care,
    The patience that he deemed he'd sought in vain.

Doubt

A doubt crept into a heart one day;
The brave heart said: "'Twill be gone tomorrow."
    Ah, little it knew!
    For it steadily grew,
Till it covered that heart with a pall of sorrow;
   And there came at length a darksome day,
   When the hope of life seemed gone for aye.

A ray of light, in a darkened heart;
Yes, only a ray, but it grew more bright,
    And it steadily spread,
    Through darkness and dread,
Till it flooded that heart with a glorious light;
   And a soul gave thanks to its God, above;
   The light was a Savior's guiding love.

The After-Glow of Pain

A youth, with proud heart, pure and strong,
    And eye with hope aflame,
Goes forth to join the busy throng,
    And win success, and fame.
He presses on, with eager feet,
    Adown the sunny way;
As yet, he knows naught of defeat,
And to the struggling ones he meets
    Gives little sympathy.

But soon the dark clouds gather 'round.
    The storm breaks overhead,
The wild winds howl, the rain comes down,
    The lightning flashes red.
But when, the last cloud swept away,
    The sun shines out again,
The youth emerges from the fray,
With softened heart, and sympathy,
    The afterglow of pain.

A maiden, full of life and love,
    Goes singing on her way;
To measured strains her light feet move,
    And joyous is her day.
A transient shade comes o'er her face,
    When told some tale of pain,
But soon a bright smile fills its place,
The song that slackened, for a space,
    Goes lightly on again.

But hark! the song at last is still;
    The smiles are changed to tears;
Dark, troubled thoughts, her young heart fill,
    And doubts, and gloomy fears.
"Ah me!" we say, "her song is o'er,
    And 'twas a joyful strain,"
But list! the maiden sings once more,
A sweeter song than e'er before,
    The afterglow of pain.

'Tis thus, 'tis thus, the infant dies,
    The parents look above;
False friends deceive us on the way,
    We seek the Greater Love.
And so the threads of grief that run
    Through life may prove our gain;
The noblest deeds that e'er were done,
The sweetest songs that e'er were sung,
    Are afterglows of pain.

If Thou Shouldst Return

If thou shouldst return with the sweet words of love,
    So earnestly spoken that day,
Methinks that thy words, this sad heart would move,
    For my pride has melted away;
And I've learned how true was the heart that I spurned,
And I've longed for the face that never returned.

If thou shouldst return to claim me thy bride,
    How gladly thy fate would I share;
How gladly I'd spend my whole life at thy side,
    How honored I'd feel to be there;
Oh, I've learned to revere the heart that I spurned!
    And I long for the face that never returned.

If thou shouldst return, ah, vain is the dream!
    I'll cherish the fancy no more;
Though dark and forsaken my pathway may seem,
I'll press bravely on as before;
    And trust in the One who forgives our mistakes,
And heals the deep wounds that our waywardness makes.

Mrs. Johnson Objects

Come right in this house, Will Johnson!
    Kin I teach you dignity?
Chasin' aft' them [po' white] children,
    Jest because you [wan' to] play.

Whut does po' white trash keer fah you?
    Want you keep away fum them;
Next, they'll be a-doin' meanness,
    An' a-givin' you the blame.

Don't come mumblin' 'bout their playthings,
    Yourn is good enough fah you;
'Twus the best that I could git you,
    An' you've got to make them do.

Go'n' to break you fum that habit,
    Yes, I am! An' mighty soon;
Next, you'll grow up like the white-folks,
    All time whinin' fah the moon.

Runnin' with them po' white children—
    Go'n' to break it up, I say!—
Pickin' up their triflin' habits,
    Soon, you'll be as spilte as they.

Come on here, an' take the baby—
    Mind now! Don't you let her fall—
'Fo' I'll have you runnin' with them,
    I won't let you play at all.

Jest set there, an' mind the baby,
    Till I tell you—You may go;
An' jest let me ketch you chasin'
    Aft' them white trash any mo'.

Parted

She said she [forgave] me;
    I looked in her eyes,
And knew that her words were true;
For one blissful moment,
    I felt my hopes rise,
And sought I, my vows to renew.

But, something I missed,
    In her calm, steady gaze,
Caused the love words to die, e'er they came;
For, though her kind heart
    So freely forgave,
Still, I knew that it was not the same.

For, once, that pure heart
    Was all but my own;
Well I knew how it quickened its beat,
How those sweet, gentle eyes,
    With a soft luster, shone,
At the sound of my coming feet.

But little I valued
    The pearl I had found,
And carelessly cast it away,
For one, whose gay laugh
    Proved a meaningless sound,
And whose heart was all vanity.

And when I returned,
    For I'd learned her true worth,
As I sadly gazed in her eyes,
I knew that her love
    Had died at its birth;
I had lost forever, my prize.

An Opening Service

"Holy, holy, holy!" the choir chants sweet and low,
    And earnest hearts are lifted up in prayer;
The organ's mellow cadence peals solemn, soft, and slow,
    And God is with His people, gathered there.

"Holy, holy, holy!" they bow before His will;
    The pastor's tones rise solemnly o'er all:—
"The Lord is in His temple, let all the earth be still."
    A deep calm reigns throughout the sacred hall.

"Holy, holy, holy!" who would not humbly bow,
    Before such holiness, such love divine?
And leaving pride and folly, join with His people, now,
    In faithful worship, at so pure a shrine.

"Holy, holy, holy!" their full hearts swell within,
    As o'er and o'er they hear the soft refrain;
And when, the service ended, the choir rings out "Amen,"
    A hundred voices mingle in the strain.

The Christmas Rush

Well, we went down town a-shopping,
    My brother and sister and I;
'Twas just two days before Christmas,
    With ev'rything yet to buy.

There were gifts for nieces and nephews,
    And trinkets for sister and me,
There were sweets for the Christmas dinner,
    And things for the Christmas tree.

We felt there was pleasure before us,
    When we cheerfully boarded the train,
But we found 'twas only business,
    Ere we reached our home again.

The streets were crowded with people,
    And at last when we reached the stores,
There was such a mass of shoppers,
    We could scarcely pass through the doors.

We forced our way to the counter,
    This bitter truth to learn—
That others were there before us,
    So we must await our turn.

At last it came, and we purchased,
    And then—'twas enough to derange!
We had the self-same experience,
    Awaiting our parcels and change.

'Twas the same at ev'ry counter;
    'Twas the same at ev'ry store;
Just pushing and crowding and waiting,
    And seemingly, nothing more.

Well, after much taxing of patience,
    Our Christmas shopping was done,
And laden with many parcels,
    We gladly started for home.

But the crowd had almost doubled,
    When we came out on the street,
And, but for the good-will of Christmas,
    We'd have lost our tempers complete.

It seemed that half of the city,
    Had come out a-shopping, that day,
While half stood at the show windows,
    To look, and to block the way.

We tried to rush—it was useless,
    Of course we missed our train,
Then waited an hour for another,
    And at last we reached home again.

And now, a few words of counsel,
    I would kindly give, by your leave,—
Don't put off your Christmas shopping,
    Till the day before Christmas eve.

An Autumn Day

I sat in the door of our cottage,
    One golden autumn day,
And the breezes stirring the tree-tops
    Were as soft as those of May.

But looking away to the woodland,
    Through hazy autumn air,
The red and gold of the forest leaves
    Proclaimed the frost-touch there.

The grass was still green in the pasture,
    Where soft-eyed cattle trod,
And down in the deep, sheltered valleys
    Were asters and golden rod.

But I knew the merciless frost-king
    Would come with might, erelong,
And blast all the green things remaining,
    And still the sweet bird-song.

So my heart drank in the warm beauty,
    Of that soft autumn day,
With a wistful love for ev'rything,
    So soon to pass away.

I'll Follow Thee

My Savior, let me hear Thy voice tonight;
    I'll follow Thee, I'll follow Thee;
The clouds that overhang my way obscure the light,
    And all is dark to me.

I'd hear Thy voice above the tempest's shriek;
    I'll follow Thee, I'll follow Thee;
And though my sight be dim, my spirit weak,
    I'll trust, though naught I see.

I'd feel Thy arm, supporting in the dark;
    I'll follow Thee, I'll follow Thee;
For Thou canst fan to flame faith's sinking spark,
    And seal my loyalty.

I shall not sink, dear Lord, when Thou'rt my guide;
    I'll follow Thee, I'll follow Thee;
Though lashed by heavy waves, on ev'ry side,
    I'm safe, when Thou'rt with me.

The Easter Light

'Tis Lent, the holy time of fast and prayer,
    Of meditation and repentant tear,
When saints bow humbly 'neath the cross they bear,
    Treading the path of duty, without fear.

But one remains within her quiet room,
    And looks with sadness out upon the town;
Lent brings her nothing to dispel the gloom,
    That hovers o'er her path, and bears her down.

What matter if the bells chime sweetly, now,
    Calling the many worshipers to prayer?
No holy light breaks o'er that clouded brow,
    She does not care to mingle with them, there.

Into her life, the hand of Death has come,
    Bearing her truest, best beloved, away;
And now, her heart, all wretched and forlorn,
    Is crying out to Death, incessantly:—

"Oh Death! give back my best beloved again;
    Give back my own, thou heartless, tyrant, king!
Seest thou my bleeding heart, all rent in twain,
    And carest thou not, that thou hast done this thing?"

'Tis Easter morn; the lenten fast is o'er;
    A risen Savior bids the glad world sing;
The grave is open; Death has pow'r no more,
    For Christ has robbed him of his deadly sting.

The church is crowded with a happy throng;
    O'er banks of flow'rs, the softened sunbeams play;
The choir bursts forth, in glad, triumphant song:
    "Oh earth, rejoice! The Lord is ris'n today."

A dark-eyed girl comes slowly down the aisle,
    Her face marked deep with bitterness and pain;
The choir is singing joyfully, the while,
    "Rejoice, rejoice! for death has ceased to reign."

The maiden lists the song, half bitterly,—
    "Well may they sing, they've never wept in vain,
They've ne'er had cause to ask, unceasingly,
    'Where shall I find my lost beloved again?'"

But listen! one is singing all alone;
    Her rich voice, welling up so full and clear,
Throbs ever, with a sad, sweet undertone,
    Telling, she, too, has met some trial here.

And now her voice sinks soft as falling dew;
    Now rising high, it seems to pierce the dome;
The undertone e'er throbbing sweet and true—
    She, too, has suffered, but has overcome.

She sings today, that some o'erburdened heart
    May find the light that shines within her own;
The maiden listens—ah! the hot tears start,
    And melts the ice that o'er her heart has grown.

The thoughtless ones gaze at her, wond'ringly:
    "How can she weep, when all the world is bright?"
While others gaze, with kindly sympathy,
    Knowing her heart has found the Easter light.

Uncle Rube on the Race Problem

How'd I solve "de Negro Problum"?
    Gentlemen, don't like dat wo'd!
'Mind me too much uv ol' slave times,
    When de white man wus de lo'd.

Spoutin' roun' about "My niggahs,"
    Knockin' us fum lef' to right,
Sellin' us, like we wus cattle,
    Drivin' us fum mawn till night,—

Oh, you say I'm off de subjec';
    Am a little off, I see,—
Well, de way to solve de problum
    Is, to let de black man be.

Say, you "fail to ketch my meanin'"?
    Now, dat's very plain to me.
Don't you know, you whites is pickin'
    On de blacks, continu'ly?

Jes' pick up de mawnin' papah,
    Anywhaur you choose to go,
When you read about de black man,
    You may bet it's somepin' low.

It's all right to tell his meanness,
    Dat's, pervided it is true;
But, why, in de name uv blazes,
    Don't you tell de good things too!

No, I ain't a-cussin' either!
    Ef my blood wus young an' waum,
Guess I'd sometimes feel like cussin',
    How you whites is takin' on.

Still, I don't hol' wid dat business,
    Leave dat, fah you whites to do—
Cussin' an' a-suicidin',
    When de whole land b'longs to you.

Den, agin, ez I wus sayin',—
    Ef a black man makes a mawk,
Seems you white-folks will go crazy,
    Try'n' to keep him in de dawk.

An', ef he don't watch his cornahs,
    An' his head ain't mighty soun',
Fust he knows: some uv you white-folks
    Done reached up, an' pulled him down.

Whut you say? I'm too hawd on you?
    Whut you 'spected me to do,
When you axed me my opinion?
    Tell you somepin' wusn't true?

Co'se dah's some exceptions 'mong you,
    An' I ain't denyin' it;
But dah's mighty few, I tell you,
    Dat kin say: "Dis shoe don't fit."

Yes, you say some blacks is "o'n'ry";
    So is many uv de whites;
But de black race mus' be perfec',
    'Fo' we git ou' "equal rights."

Foreign whites, fum ev'ry nation,
    Finds a welcome in dis lan',
Yet, dah seems to be no welcome
    Fah de native cullud man.

You don't have to "tote his skillet,"—
    Ez de folks in Dixie say,—
Only, when you see him strugglin',
    Don't you git into his way.

Co'se, ef you is got a mind to,
    You kin lend a helpin' han',
But de best help you kin give him
    Is, to treat him like a man.

Look at all de great improvement
    He has made since he wus free;
Yet, de white-folks keep a-wond'ring
    Whut's his future go'n' to be.

All time talkin' 'bout his meanness,
    An' de many things he lack,
Makin' out dey see no progress,
    Doe dey're try'n' to hol' him back.

Oh, it ain't no use in talkin',
    Ef you whites would jest play faiah,
All de wranglin' 'bout dis problum
    Soon would vanish in de aiah.

Once dey couldn't find no method
    Dat would put down slavery,
Till it like to split de country,
    Den, dey set de black man free.

Dat's de way wid dis race problum:
    Ef de white-folks had a min',
Day could fin' a answer to it,
    Like dey did de other time.

Co'se, dah's two sides to dis problum,
    An' dah's things de blacks should do,
But I'm talkin' 'bout you white-folks,
    And de pawt dat b'longs to you.

Don't know whaur to "place de black man"?
    He will fin' his place;—You'll see!
Like de foreign whites is doin',
    When you learn to let him be.

Den, you "feah amalgamation"?
    When de black man takes his stan',
Don't you know he'll squar' his shoulders,
    Proud, dat he's a Af'ican?

In dis lan', to be a black man
    Isn't called a lucky thing;
An' dat's why some fools among us
    Think it smawt to mingle in.

An' you white-folks isn't blameless,
    Some uv you is in dat too,—
Takin' ev'ry mean advantage
    Dat is in yo' powah to do.

But, de race will reach a station,
    Whaur de blindes' one kin see,
Dat 'tis good to be a black man,
    Jest ez sho' ez sho' kin be.

Den, agin, sometimes I'm thinkin'
    Dat dis 'malgamation fright's
Jes' got up by you smawt white-folks,
    Keep fum givin' us ou' rights.

Fah, ef now, in all her trials,
    Mos' uv us stick to de race,
You know well, we won't fahsake her,
    When she gits a honored place.

"Be a nation in a nation"?
    Now you're talkin' like a fool!
Whut you mean by "'Plur'bus unyun—"?
    Many nations 'neath one rule.

Not go'n' back on dat ol' motto,
    Dat has made yo' country's name,
Jest because de race you brung here
    Ax you fah a little claim?

Well, I 'spec' I mus' be goin',
    Gittin' kinder late, I see;
Guess nex' time "Ol' Rube" is passin',
    Gentlemen, you'll let him be.

Oh, you say, "you bah no malice"?
    Well, I'd ruther have it so,
But I'll hol' up fah my people,
    Whethah folks like it or no.

Hope Deferred

"There's light ahead!" Hope ever cries;
    I onward press, in better cheer;
But when I reach the fancied goal,
I find, the wind blows fierce and cold,
    The place is dark and drear.
I, falt'ring, sink, with courage gone;
But Hope cries ever, "Onward, on!"

I rise, and onward press again,
    Still looking for the promised light;
The wind, the mist, the blinding rain
Come sweeping o'er the barren plain,
    And all is dark as night.
I grope—I cannot find the way;
Hope whispers of a brighter day.

So on, and ever on, I press,
    With weary heart, and aching feet;
Hope strives in vain to cheer the way,
With promise of a coming day,
    When life will be more sweet.
I cannot listen to her song,
The night is dark, the way is long.
    A bitterness comes o'er my soul,
I cry, beneath the gloom,
    Oh Hope, thou seemest but a myth,
To lure us to our doom!

Church Bells

I closed my book to listen;
    The story was losing its charms,
As the chime of distant church bells
    Came stealing o'er gardens and farms.
The bells were chiming a story,
    A story that ne'er grows old:
The story of Christ, our Shepherd,
    And the sweet peace found in His fold,
The story of all He suffered,
    That we might have a home;
And now, the bells were calling
    The weary ones, to come;
The bells were calling, calling,—
    Blest, tender, pleading tone!
"Oh weary ones," they sweetly chimed,
    "Oh weary ones, come home."

The birds flew past the window,
    With twitter and flutter and song,
Their hearts o'erflowing with music,
    Glad hearts, that knew no wrong;
But the far-off bells were chiming,
    Of a price paid long ago,
That we, through faith, may be sinless,
    And pure as the falling snow.
"Come thou, oh weary pilgrim,
    With burden grown too great,
Thy Savior now is waiting,
    Oh, lay them at His feet!"

The bells were calling, calling,—
    Blest, gentle, pleading tone!
"Oh weary ones, oh weary ones,
    Oh weary ones, come home."

Hath sin thy hands been staining,
    Until they're pure no more?
Hath thorns thy feet been piercing,
    Until they're bleeding sore?
Come thou to Christ, thy Savior;
    His hand is stretched to thee.
Take it; 'twill guide thee safe thro' life,
    And through eternity.
Sweetly, the bells are calling;
    Oh sinner, heed the tone!
"Oh wicked ones, oh wand'ring ones,
    Oh weary ones, come home."

Thou canst not be too wretched,
    To heed the gentle call;
Thou canst not be too wicked,—
    His blood was shed for all;
Though scoffers by the wayside
    Scorn those who heed the tone,
The bells chime clear and sweetly,—
    "Thrice blest are they;—come home."
The bells are calling, calling,—
    "Tired sinner, wilt thou come?
Oh wretched ones, oh weeping ones,
    Oh weary ones, come home."

List ye! the tones are changing;
    Hark! 'tis thy Savior's voice,
Yes, 'tis thy Savior calling,
    And wilt thou make thy choice?
Why dost thou vainly struggle
    To bear thy load alone,
When such a Friend is waiting,
    When such a Friend says, "Come"?
Thy Savior's waiting—pleading:
    "Oh weary, wilt thou come?
Oh weary ones, oh burdened ones,
    Oh weary ones, come home."

She Sent Him Away

She sent him away, with no word of love,
    Though he'd wooed her many a day,
And she knew that his heart was all her own,
    Yet, she coldly sent him away.

She sent him away, with his pleading eyes,
    And heeded not look, nor tone,
But chained down her heart, when it struggled to rise
    In response to the love in his own.

But when he had gone far, far from her side,
    She found,—ah, lamentable day!—
That her heart had broken the chain of pride,
    And followed her lover away.

Out of the Deep
A Prayer

Out of the deep, I cry to Thee, oh Lord!
    Out of the deep of darkness and distress;
I cannot, will not doubt Thy blessed word,
    Oh, God of righteousness!

I cry, and oh, my God, I know Thou'lt heed,
    For Thou hast promised Thou wouldst heed my cry;
I have no words to tell my deepest need,
    Thou knowest oh, Most High!

Thou knowest all the pain,—the agony,
    The grief I strive so vainly to express;
Oh let Thy shelt'ring wings spread over me,
    Great God of tenderness!

I cannot, cannot cease to cry to Thee,
    For oh, my God, this heart is not my own,
And as the streams press ever to the sea,
    My heart turns to Thy throne.

And when, too weak to lift my voice, I lie
    In utter silence at Thy blessed feet,
Thou'lt know that silence is my deepest cry,
    Thy throne, my last retreat.

And shouldst Thou hide Thy face for aye, from me,
    My heart, though shattered, evermore would grope
Out through the darkness, still in search of Thee,
    Oh God, my only hope!

Uncle Rube to the Young People

Press ahead, beloved children!
    Doe I will be dead an' gone,
Dah is great things waitin' fah you,
    Jest as sho' as you is bawn.

Yeahs ago,—'way back in slave times,
    'Fo' it seemed sech things could be,
Some ole people use to whispah,
    Dat some day, we would be free.

P'r'aps dey heard de white-folks talkin',
    Who wus lookin' fah ahead;
P'r'aps dey'd axed de Lo'd about it,
    An' wus tellin' whut He'd said.

Anyhow, de way wus dawker
    Fah de race, dan 'tis today,
Yet, dey saw de light a-comin',
    Doe it wus so fah away.

So don't b'lieve de Lo'd's fahsook us,
    An' will no mo' show His face;
Ef He wus dat stern a Fathah,
    He done killed de whole white race.

Take new courage, den, my children,
    Don't lose faith, whute'er you do;
Ef He's patient wid de white-folks,
    He'll be patient wid us too.

Co'se we mus'n't 'pose upon Him,
    But mus' do de bes' we kin;
An' remembah dis, my children,
    Dat He wants us to be men.

Don't spend all yo' time a-parl'in'
    Whethah things is right er wrong,
Ax de Lo'd to guide yo' footsteps,
    Den, git up, an' go right on.

Some folks ax de Lo'd to guide dem,
    Den, when He p'ints out de way,
'Stid uv goin' on, a-trustin',
    Keep a ling'ring back, to pray;

'Case dey think it safer, kneelin'
    In some secret, sheltahed place,
Whaur de enemy can't find dem,
    Dan to meet him, face to face.

But I wan' to tell you children,
    Dat I know dis, fah a fac':
Ef you do dat kin' uv prayin',
    Things is go'n' to go to wrack.

'Case it ain't no use in talkin',
    None uv us kin fool de Lo'd;
When we do dat lazy prayin',
    He ain't go'n' to hear a wo'd.

Humph! we kin go on a-prayin'
    Dat fool way, yeah aftah yeah,
An' we'll fin' de same ole bothah—
    Dat de Lo'd ain't go'n' to heah.

'Way back—in de days uv slav'ry,
    Folks done nothin' else, but pray;
Den, deir feet an' hands wus fettahed,
    An' dey saw no othah way.

But de Lo'd has broke de fettahs,
    An' de times has changed since den,
So dis younger generation
    Mus' git up, an' act like men.

Don't spend all yo' time a-frettin',
    'Case de white-folks spile yo' chance;
Ef you's got de propah courage,
    Min'! dey can't check yo' advance.

Co'se, dey'll give a sight uv trouble,
    Since dey's fo'most in de land,
But de re'l fate uv ou' nation
    Isn't in de white-folks' hands.

So you needn't feah dem, children,
    Don't fahgit whut David said;—
"Lo'd's my strength an' my life giver;
    Uv whom shell I be afraid?"

Ef you take dis fah yo' motto,
    You will fin',—whute'er you do,
Ef it's fah yo' life's up buildin',
    Dat de Lo'd will help you through.

An', another thing, my children,
    Don't git dis into yo' head,—
Dat, all dat He wants to give us
    Is a little meat an' bread.

Fah, I've learnt dis, in my life-time:
    Dat de Lo'd is bounteous,
An' He'll do great big things fah us,
    Ef we only learn to trus'.

Co'se, it's all right to be 'umble,
    Pride will often spile success,
But some people say dey's 'umble,
    When it's only shiftlessness.

Not a-tryin' to be successful;
    Puttin' up wid anything;
An' when othah people prospah,
    Makin' out dat it's a sin.

Mind de par'ble uv de talents?
    How de man dat had but one,
Went an' dug a hole, an' hid it,
    Waitin', till de mastah come?

Makin' out he feahed to use it,
    Said his mastah wusn't jus',
An' ef he should make a blundah,
    When he come, he'd make a fuss.

'Membah, when de mastah did come,
    How he took dat man to tes'?
How he took his talent fum him,
    Fah his lazy shiftlessness?

Don't you be like dat bad servant,
    Even ef yo' chance is small;
Don't git lazy an' discouraged,
    An' jest make no show at all.

Fah de Lo'd'll increase yo' chances,
    When He sees you've done yo' bes',
But ef you refuse to use dem,
    Some day, He'll take you to tes'.

Now I ain't a-quar'lin' children,
    Doe my words may kinder goad;
I'm jes' p'intin' out de pitfalls,
    Dat you'll find along de road.

Fah dah's many uv dem, children,
    An', one uv de wust I know,
Is dis dreadful inclernation,
    Jest to set and let things go.

Spite uv all de odds agin us,
    Dah's a heap dat we kin do,
Things dat don't concern de white-folks,
    Things dat b'long to me an' you:

Learnin' to respect each othah;
    Holdin' up fah ou' own race;
And a-keepin' down ou' envy,
    When one gains a higher place.

Learnin' how to use ou' jedgement,
    'Bout de things dat come along,
'Stid uv waitin' till de white-folks
    Say ef it is right er wrong.

Keepin' faith in ou' own people,
    Doe dey make us sick at hawt,
Wid deir weakness an' deir folly,
    While dey're try'n' to git a stawt.

Fah dese great an' mighty nations,
 Dat's now rulin' land and sea,
Stawted out on next to nothin',
 Jest de same ez you and me.

An' I'm not a-boastin' children,
 Fah I know my people's worth:—
Dah's ez good a stuff in ou' race,
 Ez in any race on earth.

But de race needs cultivation;
 I don't keer how rich de soil,
It ain't go'n' to bring forth produce
 Fah its ownah, 'less he toil.

Dat is why I keep a-sayin',
 To you, ovah an' agin,
Dat we's bound to quit ou' foolin',
 And git up and act like men.

Now, dis sounds like modern doctrine,
 Fah a ole-time chap like me,
But I had my own opinions,
 Even 'fo' dey set me free.

White-folks called me "Mistah Hawd-head,"
 And dey'd knock and cuff me roun',
But, in spite uv all de beatin',
 Dey jes' couldn't keep me down.

An' soon ez de Good News reached us,
 (Jiniwary, sixty three,)
I lit out an' jined de ahmy,
 An dey saw no mo' uv me

So I've been a-tryin' children,
    Evah since, to help my race,
Doe, sometimes I do so little,
    I'm 'mos' 'shamed to show my face.

But, doe we can't all be leaders,
    We kin do de best we kin,
An' dis is my pray'r dear children,
    May God help us to be men!

The Skeptic

Written on an Incident, Read in a Periodical

The mother's face looked tired and worn,
    While speaking of her son;
The good man listened earnestly,
    As she went sadly on,

Telling of days of weariness,
    And nights of earnest prayer,
All, all for him, whose soul had been
    Her heart's most anxious care.

"You'll speak to him?" at last, she said.
    "Perhaps, your clearer sight
Will find a way, I have not seen,
    To lead him to the Light."

"God helping me," the list'ner said,
    And went to seek her son.
He found the young man hard and cold,
    With heart that bowed to none.

He "knew not if there were a God,"
    He said, with careless pride—
"What know I, positive, of Christ,
    Or that He lived and died?"

He doubted all the prophecies,
    And ev'ry Bible truth;
He had no faith in God nor man,
    This proud, rebellious youth.

The good man paused,—he knew of naught,
    That this man's heart would move;
At last, he asked, if he had faith,
    In his good mother's love.

The dark look left those doubting eyes;
    "That love, so deep and pure,
How could I doubt?" he quickly said.
    "Of that, I'm always sure."

"You say, you will not pray to God,
    Because I cannot prove;
Then, will you breathe one earnest prayer,
    This night, my boy, to love?"

The young man promised; in his heart,
    He sadly craved for light;
His promise filled his mind again,
    When all alone that night;

And, kneeling down, within his room,
    He whispered low: "Oh, Love!"
There came unto his waiting heart,
    The answer: "God is Love."

And then, his heart cried low: "Oh God!"
    The answer came again:—
"Because of God's all-pitying love,
    The blessed Savior came."

Then,—then went up the yearning cry:—
    "Oh, Christ, Thou Love Divine,
Shed Thou the light of Thy great Truth,
    O'er this dark heart of mine!"

His heart stood still, in ecstasy;
    The blessed Light had come;
He rose, with joy, unspeakable,
    And sought his mother's room.

A Lullaby

Hush ye, hush ye! honey, darlin',
    Hush ye, now, an' go to sleep;
Mammy's got to wash them dishes,
    An' she's got this floor to sweep.

You must think I'm made uv money,
    An's got nothin' else to do,
But to set here, in this rocker,
    Like a lady, holdin' you.

Now you's gone to laughin' at me;
    Little rascal! Hush! I say,
Mammy's got to wash them dishes,
    She ain't got no time to play.

Ef you don't quit lookin' at me,
    With that little sassy eye,
I declare, I'll tell your daddy,
    An' tonight, he'll make you fly.

Now jest look how you's a-laughin'!
    See you's bound to have your way,
I'll jest have to set an' hold you;
    Won't git nothin' done today.

The Empty Tomb

    Calv'ry's tragedy is ended;
        They have laid Him in the tomb,
And with jealous care, His enemies have sealed it;
        But they cannot keep Him there,
        For an earthquake rends the air,
And an angel rolls away the stone that closed it.

    None are there to greet the Savior,
        As He leaves the open tomb;
All forgotten are the promises He gave them;
        And the women wend their way
        To the tomb, ere it is day;
Not in faith, for death's sad emblems bring they with them.

    Oh, the darkness of that morning,
        When they stood before His tomb,
With the spices and the ointments to anoint Him!
        And I hear sad Mary say,
        "They have taken Him away,
And I know not, and I know not where they've laid Him."

    Oh, ye ones of faithless doubting!
        Know ye not what Jesus said,
While in life, His toil to you was freely given?
        Now ye stand, with hearts of woe,
        While your bitter tears doth flow,
Knowing not your Lord and Savior has arisen.

Then the Savior speaks to Mary,
    And at first, she knows Him not,
For her eyes are darkened by her doubts and sadness.
    Then, He speaks to her again,
    Gently calls her by her name.
And she greets her risen Lord with wondrous gladness.

Often in the Christians' struggle,
    When the battle rages sore,
And on ev'ry side the bitter foes assail them,
    E'en like her, they sadly say:—
    "They have taken Him away,
And I know not, and I know not where they've laid Him."

And, like her, with bitter weeping,
    As they face the empty tomb,
All His promises and wondrous deeds forgotten,
    If they'd turn, they'd find Him near,
    With such loving words of cheer,
That they'd know 'twas doubt, that made them feel forsaken.

Drift-Wood

They brought in the brine-crusted drift-wood,
    And heaped it high on the hearth,
For the snow, outside, was falling fast,
    And the winter wind was wroth.

I watched the bright flames leaping upward,
    As the drift-wood flashed and burned,
And I mused on the fate of those who sailed
    In the ship, that ne'er returned.

My fancy then wrought out two stories,
    And one was sad and drear:
Of lashing waves and struggling souls,
    And piercing cries of fear.

The other was bright and hopeful:
    For the wild waves lost their prey,
When a stately ship came gliding by,
    And bore the crew away.

Then, musing on my fancies,
    I wondered which one bore
The truer tale of the good ship, cast
    As drift-wood, on the shore.

Submission

I'll faint no more beneath the burden
    My Lord has given me to bear;
What matter if my heart is laden,
    And sadness finds a refuge there?

He promised not unbroken gladness,
    If we would trace His bleeding feet,
But strength to bear life's toil and sadness,
    To overcome the foes we meet.

What matter if the way be narrow?
    We have His loving sympathy;
Did He not tread earth's path of sorrow,
    From Bethlehem to Calvary?

And are we better than the Master,
    Who bore for us mortality?
Or wiser than the Heavenly Father,
    Whose great love suffered this to be?

I'll trust the God, whose great compassion
Sent to Gethsemane His Son,
    Who shamed forever our rebellion,
When there He prayed:—"Thy will be done."

The Angel's Message

There's a wonderful story,
    That never grows old,
Though centuries have passed,
    Since first it was told;
Since the angel of God,
    On that far, early morn,
Proclaimed to the shepherds,
    That Jesus was born.
Ah, the news was too great
    For poor mortal to bring!
An angel must tell
    Of the birth of the King.

The people of God
    Had long looked for His Son,
The prophets had said:
    "He surely will come;
Jehovah has promised
    His own Son to give,
To suffer and die,
    That His people may live."
And the angels were first
    The glad tidings to bring:
"Glory to God in the highest,
    He has sent thee thy King!"

The wondering shepherds
    Cast out all their fears,
When the angels' glad tidings
    Rang sweet in their ears,
And leaving their flocks,
    Into Bethlehem went,

And beheld the great Gift
    Their Father had sent.
In a Bethlehem stable
    The little One lay:
His cradle, the manger;
    His pillow, the hay.

The bright star of promise
    Was seen in the east,
And then, to the manger
    Came prophet and priest;
Came hither the wise men,
    Rich presents to bring,
And worship this Infant,
    Their Savior and King.
Then returned to their land
    By a devious way,
That the king might not know
    Where the little One lay.

Now, when they'd departed,
    An angel of light
Appeared unto Joseph,
    Slumbering at night:
"Arise! take the Child
    And His mother, and fly;
King Herod decrees
    That the Infant must die."

And Joseph and Mary
    Fled off in the night,
With Christ, our Redeemer,
    From Herod's grim might;

Into Egypt they went
    With the pure Holy One;
Oh, the Father knew well
    How to guard His dear Son!
The Son He so loved,
    But freely did give,
To die, that the whole world
    Might look up, and live.

Ah no! that sweet story
    Can never grow old,
Though long years have passed,
    Since first it was told;
Since first the glad angels
    Sang sweet its refrain,
And now we repeat it
    Again and again:—
"Glory to God in the highest,
    For the dear Savior's birth!
Glory to God in the highest,
    And peace upon earth!"
And down through the ages,
    That chorus shall ring,
Till earth's ev'ry nation
    Crowns Jesus its King.

Storm-Beaten

Weary, worn, and sorrow-laden,
    Jesus, I have come to Thee;
Shield me from the darts of Satan;
    Set my fettered spirit free.

Hearken to my plea for guidance,
    As I kneel before Thy throne;
Cheer me with Thy Holy Presence,
    When I feel I'm all alone.

Struggling with the cares that press me,
    Falling, when I fain would stand,
Thou alone, canst guide and keep me,
    Take, oh take my trembling hand!

Pity Thou my many failings;
    Strengthen Thou my falt'ring trust;
Keep me, 'mid the wind's loud wailing,
    Thou, the Pitiful and Just!

The Old and the New

"Son, come tell me 'bout the meetin';
    Kinder glad I didn't go,
Since the night turned out so stormy,
    Feels alike it's go'n' to snow.

"I've been settin' here, a-noddin',
    An' a-listenin' to the win';
Jest 'bout dropped off in a slumber,
    When I heard you comin' in.

"Wus the sermon good this ev'nin'?
    ('Spec' 'twus jest about the same;)
We ain't had no rousin' sermons,
    Since that Elder Ma'shall came."

"Well, you'll have to change that, mother,
    Marshall tried himself tonight;
My! the women got to shouting,
    And they knocked things left and right.

"Mother, you just ought to've been there."
    "Wush I had! I'us 'bout to say:—
Something's always sure to happen,
    Ev'ry time I stay away.

"Go on, tell me all about it."
    "Can't begin to tell you all,
But that Smith girl near went crazy,
    And she got an awful fall.

"Five or six were trying to hold her,
    But that woman pitched and tore,
Till at last, she broke loose from them,
    And fell flat, on that hard floor.

"Tell you, ma, it kind of scared me;
    When she fell, she struck her head,
And she lay so stiff and quiet,
    That it seemed like she was dead."

"Wouldn't 'a' happened ef I'd been there,
    Guess they didn't hold her tight;
But it won't be nothin' ser'ous,
    Ef the gal wus shoutin' right."

"I'm not sure about that, mother."
    "Well, I am! and now, go on;
Tell me mo' about the meetin',
    For I see 'twus p'int'ly wawm.

"Wush to goodness, I had been there!
    Serves me right! that's what I got,
Settin' by the fire a sleepin';
    Could 'a' gone as well as not.

"I jest know Aunt Luce got happy!"
    "Ma, you've never seen her shout!
Why, she just did take on awful,
    And Florinda took her out."

"Took her out? Jest like Florinda!
    She's entirely too high-tone';
Gittin' 'shamed uv her old grandma;
    Think she'd better left her 'lone."

"Mother, I don't blame Florinda,
    For Aunt Luce is pretty old,
And the church was all confusion,
    Seemed they'd got beyond control."

"I don't keer! it wouldn't hurt her,
    Ef she'd let her had it out;
That's some more uv your new notions;
    Folks don't git too old to shout."

"Now, I didn't say that mother."
    "Think I don't know what you mean?
You wus gittin' down on shoutin'
    Long before you left your teens."

"Didn't say I hated shouting,
    Sometimes, it may be all right;
But they often overdo it,
    And that's what they did tonight."

"Oh don't talk 'bout overdoin'.
    You can't smooth it over none,
Ef you had your way about it,
    'Twouldn't be no shoutin' done.

"Talkin' 'bout them overdoin'!
    Ef you had a mite uv sense,
You would know they couldn't help it;
    They can't stop, once they commence."

"Oh that's what they always tell you!
    I know that old song by heart;
If they know they can't control it,
    Then they'd better not to start.

"Acting like they'd lost their senses;
    Don't care how far they're behind
In their common sense and business,
    So they have that 'happy time.'

"When it comes to noise and shouting,
    Plenty answer to the call;
When it's work, and sober thinking,
    Then, a few must do it all."

"Shame on you! Your ma has shouted,
    An' you know she'll shout agin;
Shucks! I thought you had religion,
    But I see you're still in sin."

"Why I didn't mean you, mother;
    You think I'd say that of you?"
"Boy, ef you don't b'lieve in shoutin',
    I don't know whut you would do!"

"Oh, I wish I hadn't spoken!
    Ma, you don't quite understand—"
"'Spec' I don't; I'm so old-fashioned,
    An' you're such a modern man,

"With your high-flown modern notions
    'Bout the way the church should go;
Comin' here a-scornin' shoutin'!
    You must think that I am Flo.

"No, indeed! I ain't Florinda;
    Since she come back fum that school,
An' you've been a courtin' uv her,
    Don't know which's the biggest fool.

"'Spec' when you an' her git married,
    You won't have me 'round you, then;
'Spec' you'll send me to the po' house,
    Ef I dare to say 'Amen.'"

"Ma, you know you're talking nonsense,
    I'd been married long ago,
If I hadn't been a waiting
    Till you learn to care for Flo.

"And you're too hard on Florinda;
    'Course, she doesn't shout and scream,
But a truer, sweeter Christian,
    I, for one, have never seen.

"Why, I wouldn't give Florinda,
    With her gentle, Christian way,
For a dozen shouting women,
    Can't help what you old folks say!"

"Nonsense! boy, you's gone plumb crazy;
    I kin git along with Flo,
Go on, mar'y her ef you wan' to,—
    Might of told me that befo'.

"So that's where the shoe is pinchin'?
    Waitin' see whut I would do;
'Fraid I won't git 'long with Flora;
    Boy, don't I git 'long with you?

"You is jest as bad as Flora,
    Both is got your high-tone' ways,
Aftah all, 'spec' you can't help it,
    Comin' 'long in these new days.

"Well, we won't quar'l 'bout religion,
    Folks an' times change like the tide;
But your ma will keep on shoutin',
    Till she reach the 'other side.'"

Oh List to My Song!

Oh list to my song, my sweet, dark eyed dove!
    Oh list to thy lover today!
For I've come from afar, to woo thee again,
    Though, erstwhile, you sent me away.

But I heard thy sighs in my troubled dreams,
    And methought they were sighs of pain;
So I've come, I've come on the wings of my love,
    To offer my true heart again.

Oh say that my heart has not hoped in vain!
    Oh tell me the sweet dream was true!
And lift those dark lashes, oh sweet love of mine,
    And hide not thine eyes from my view.

Oh love, those dear eyes are telling the tale,
    That thy lips refuse to repeat!
Come thou, to my heart; thou art mine, thou art mine,
    Till time and eternity meet!

Not Dead, But Sleeping

We say he is dead; ah, the word is too somber;
    'Tis the touch of God, on the weary eyes,
That has caused them to close, in peaceful slumber,
    To open with joy, in the upper skies.

We say he is gone; we have lost him forever;
    His face and his form we will cherish no more;
While happy and safe, just over the river,
    He is waiting for us, where partings are o'er.

Ah, sad are our hearts, as we gaze on him sleeping,
    And bitter and sad are the tears gushing down;
And yet,—but we cannot see, for the weeping,—
    He has only exchanged the cross, for the crown.

And though the dark mists of grief may surround us,
    Obscuring the face of the Father above,
And blindly we grope, still His arms are around us,
    To guide and sustain with His pitying love

And he whom we love is safe in His keeping,
    Yes, safe and secure, whatever may come;
But ne'er will we know how sweetly he's sleeping,
    Till God, in His mercy, shall gather us home.

The Easter Bonnet

John, look what Mis' Nelson give me,
    When I cleaned for her today;
Mean, close-fisted, old white woman!
    'Clare, I'll throw the thing away!

You may just say I've gone crazy,
    When I wear a thing like that;
Just look at that 'bomination!
    Who would call that thing a hat?

What say? "Beggars can't be choosers"?
    Didn't ask her for the thing—
Only said that Easter's coming,
    An' I'd need a hat this spring.

Then she went upstairs a-prancing,
    And I looked for something grand;
Next I knew, she come down, grinning,
    With this fool thing in her hand.

Guess she knew I didn't like it,
    For I just made out to say:
"Much obliged to you Mis' Nelson,—"
    Got right up and come away.

John, I saw hats in her closet,
    That she only bought last year,
An' says now they're out of fashion,
    That I'd be too glad to wear.

But she would'nt give them to me,
    'Fraid I'd hold my head too high;
Giving me this old-time bonnet!
    'Clare, I'm mad enough to cry.

"Oh, don't mind old Mrs. Nelson,
    Been an old fool all her life;
I'll buy you your Easter bonnet;
    She don't have to clothe my wife.

"But I can't help laughing, Jennie,
    When I see that turned-up nose;
Ha! ha! ha! guess you'll quit hinting
    For the white-folks' cast-off clothes."

Autumn Leaves

Oh, the gorgeous leaves of autumn!
    Waking long-forgotten dreams
Of the days of early childhood,
    When we gayly gathered them;

Wove them into bright-hued chaplets,
    Placed them on a childish brow,
Dreaming dreams of fame and fortune,
    That we smile to think of now.

Or, with ever fertile fancy,
    Traced we fairy castles fine,
Flowing brooks, and winding rivers,
    In each varied tint and line.

Or we gazed in childish wonder,
    While the trees in beauty shone,
Red and purple, gold and russet,
    Each with beauty all its own.

And the branches gently swaying
    In the soft October breeze,
Gave fresh treasures to our keeping—
    Golden, bright-hued, autumn leaves.

Now we've left those days behind us,
    And we face the sober life,
All our childish dreams and fancies,
    Lost beneath its toil and strife.

But whene'er comes bright October,
    With her wealth of golden trees,
Then again, we're dreaming children,
    Playing in the autumn leaves.

The Watcher

A faithful watcher sits alone,
    And waits to see the Old Year die;
And sober are the thoughts that come,
    As silently the hours slip by:—

The dear Old Year is almost gone;
    Full soon I'll say a sad "Farewell";
I ask myself, what good I've done;
What deeds of love have I to tell?

Have I been patient, kind, and just,
    Forgiving, loving, faithful, true,
During the year that dies tonight,
    And yields his scepter to the New.

Perchance, I have more patient been,
    More faithful, than in years now gone,
But, ah, I've greater heights to win,
    Trusting the Grace that leads me on.

And this, my pray'r tonight shall be,
    While glad bells chime: "The guest is here."
Oh, gracious Father, guide Thou me,
    And keep Thy children through this year!

The watcher ends his simple pray'r,
    And lo! a deep peace tills his soul;
He fearless greets the glad New Year,
    For God, the Father, has control.

APPENDIX A

Editing Corrections

EDITING CORRECTIONS

AARON BELFORD THOMPSON, HARVEST OF THOUGHTS

[MS] = *Mornings Songs* (1899)
[ES] = *Echoes of Spring* (1901)

Poem	Line	Page	Original Text	Alternate Text	Corrected Text (This Edition)
A Bright Reflection	34	4	**There** mothers kind,		**Their** mothers kind
A Bright Reflection	43	4	We bear **life'** burden sheaf,		We bear **life's** burden sheaf,
A Message	11	5	**Decending** it seemed from the tree tops,		**Descending** it seemed from the tree tops,
Lines to Autumn	21	9	Oh **autumn**! whither comest thou [See line 9.]		Oh **Autumn**! whither comest thou
A Plea to the Muse	17	12	Then a bright glittering **ra inbow decended** from heaven,		Then a bright glittering **rainbow descended** from heaven,
A Plea to the Muse	42	13	**Decending** the vale of Mt. Calvary's Steep.		**Descending** the vale of Mt. Calvary's Steep.
Night	7	15	With her jet black **curley** hair,	With her jet black **curling** hair, [ES]	With her jet black **curly** hair,

EDITING CORRECTIONS

Poem	Line	Page	Original Text	Alternate Text	Corrected Text (This Edition)
An Ode to Ireland	7	17	Of her **worriors** tried, who wielded the **swoard**,	Of her **warriors** tried, who wielded the **sword**, [ES]	Of her **warriors** tried, who wielded the **sword**,
An Ode to Ireland	11	17	Her **cheiftains**, who headed her men on the field,	Her **chieftains**, who headed her men on the field, [ES]	Her **chieftains**, who headed her men on the field,
An Ode to Ireland	16	17	'Twould be such a **balad**, the world never knew.	'Twould be such a **ballad**, the world never knew. [ES]	'Twould be such a **ballad**, the world never knew.
Santa Claus' Sleigh Ride	4	18	And took up the **reigns** in his sleigh.	And took up the **reins** in his sleigh. [ES]	And took up the **reins** in his sleigh.
Santa Claus' Sleigh Ride	20	18	He **'gan** mounted roofs overhead.	He **'gain** mounted roofs overhead. [ES]	He **'gain** mounted roofs overhead.
A Christmas Carol	2	20	While shepherds did watch their **floocks** on the green;	While shepherds did watch their **flocks** on the green, [ES]	While shepherds did watch their **flocks** on the green,
A Christmas Carol	14	20	Went forth to that city, and **Jesue** they found;	Went forth to that city and **Jesus** they found;	Went forth to that city, and **Jesus** they found;
The Chiming Bells	11	22	And oft when at the **alter** stood,	And oft when at the **alter** stood, [MS]	And oft when at the **altar** stood,

EDITING CORRECTIONS

Poem	Line	Page	Original Text	Alternate Text	Corrected Text (This Edition)
A Proposal	26	24	Let **you** head lean on my bres';	Let **yo'** head lean on my breast [ES]	Let **yo'** head lean on my bres';
A Proposal	28	24	I's so gled **yo'** answered "YES!"	I's so gled **yo'** answered "YES!" [ES]	I's so gled **you** answered "Yes"!
A Birthday Tribute	3	26	She has reached each year a **mile stone**, [See line 21.]	She have reached each year a **milestone**, [MS]	She has reached each year a **milestone**,
A Birthday Tribute	8	26	As the **mile stones** pass away. [See line 21.]	As the **milestones** pass away. [MS]	As the **milestones** pass away.
Our Girls	1	28	A song to the damsel, our Ethiope **miad**!	A song to the damsels,our Ethiope **maids**! [MS]	A song to the damsel, our Ethiope **maid**!
Our Girls	15	28	Arrayed in her beauty, our **maids** we will bring.	Arrayed in her beauty,our **maids** we will bring.	Arrayed in her beauty, our **maid** we will bring.
To Helen	15	33	From wounded love in deep **dispair**,	From wounded love in deep **dispair**, [ES]	From wounded love in deep **despair**;
To Helen	20	33	**An** hear my song of love.	**And** hear my song of love. [ES]	**And** hear my song of love.
Tale of the Haunted Dell	10	34	With **firey** eyes and hideous frown,		With **fiery** eyes and hideous frown,

EDITING CORRECTIONS

Poem	Line	Page	Original Text	Alternate Text	Corrected Text (This Edition)
Tale of the Haunted Dell	11	34	**Defyantly** loud do they yell.		**Defiantly** loud do they yell.
Tale of the Haunted Dell	24	35	'Tis said **and** old poet once heard of that spot,		'Tis said **an** old poet once heard of that spot,
Tale of the Haunted Dell	106	38	**Atlength** the old pilgrim finished his song,		**At length** the old pilgrim finished his song;
Tale of the Haunted Dell	107	38	Then handing the golden **scrole,**		Then handing the golden **scroll,**
A Deserted Homestead	26	39	Once flourished with **southorn** grace,	Once flourished with **southorn** grace,	Once flourished with **southern** grace,
A Deserted Homestead	63	41	Whose **grandure** and splendor had faded,	Whose **grandure** and splendor had faded, [ES]	Whose **grandeur** and splendor had faded.
A Deserted Homestead	64	41	The pages of wealth all **eraced.**	The pages of wealth all **eraced.** [ES]	The pages of wealth all **erased.**
Miss Susie's Social	2	46	That took place at Susie **Greenes'?** [See line 47.]	That took place at Susie **Greenes'?** [ES]	That took place at Susie **Green's?**
Miss Susie's Social	73	48	So between these three fine **coupels,**	So between these three fine **coupels,** [ES]	So between these three fine **couples,**

273

EDITING CORRECTIONS

Poem	Line	Page	Original Text	Alternate Text	Corrected Text (This Edition)
Boyhood Days	45	51	My heart was glad but **its** growing sad,		My heart was glad but **it's** growing sad,
Boyhood Days	48	51	Few, few are the lads that **Iknow,**		Few, few are the lads that **I know.**
The Bachelor's Soliloquy	title	52	The Bachelor's **Soliloqy**	The Bachelor's **Soliloquy**	The Bachelor's **Soliloquy**
Fritz Mohler's Dream	5	53	Bill **Wickman's** bar was crowded, [See line 10.]	Bill **Wickmann's** bar was crowded; [ES]	Bill **Wickmann's** bar was crowded,
Fritz Mohler's Dream	6	53	With loafers **boistous** loud;	With loafers **boistrous** loud; [ES]	With loafers **boistrous** loud;
Fritz Mohler's Dream	14	53	To white-folks standing **'rouud;**	The white fo'kes stood **around;** [ES]	To white-folks standing **'round;**
Fritz Mohler's Dream	18	53	To card and **billard** game,	To card and **billiard** game, [ES]	To card and **billiard** game,
Fritz Mohler's Dream	20	53	**Fitz** Mohler was his name: [See line 41.]	**Fritz** Mohler was his name. [ES]	**Fritz** Mohler was his name:

EDITING CORRECTIONS

Poem	Line	Page	Original Text	Alternate Text	Corrected Text (This Edition)
Fritz Mohler's Dream	37	54	Sang something '**bont** the crow and crane,	Sang something '**bout** the crow and crane, [ES]	Sang something '**bout** the crow and crane,
Fritz Mohler's Dream	109	56	A thream be sometimes vot **its** not,	A thream be sometimes vot **its** not; [ES]	A thream be sometimes vot **it's** not;
The Same Old Sun	17	58	And at the **Jordon** river,	And at the **Jordan** river, [MS]	And at the **Jordan** river,
The Same Old Sun	48	59	Come, see where He has **layed**."	Come, see where He hath **layed**." [MS]	Come, see where He has **laid**."
Tale of the Wind	7	61	Saw **hue** trees 'neath thy dominions	Saw **huge** trees 'neath thy dominions [ES]	Saw **huge** trees 'neath thy dominions
Reason Why I's Happy	2	64	I's gwine 'o marry? coase **its** so!		I's gwine 'o marry? coase **it's** so!
Down Murray's Hall	15	65	**Their** came a crowd from the West Fork Side;	**There** came a crowd from the West Fork Side; [ES]	**There** came a crowd from the West Fork Side,
Down Murray's Hall	20	65	For a **nickle** a head, down Murray's hall,	For a **nickle** a head, down Murray's hall, [ES]	For a **nickel** a head down Murray's hall,
Down Murray's Hall	90	68	His loud doleful voice rang out through the **hall**,	His loud doleful voice rang out through the **hall**, [ES]	His loud doleful voice rang out through the **hall**,

EDITING CORRECTIONS

Poem	Line	Page	Original Text	Alternate Text	Corrected Text (This Edition)
Down Murray's Hall	102	68	**Sill** John Lee fiddled, an' Jim Cross called,	**Still** John Lee fiddled an' Jim Cross called, [ES]	**Still** John Lee fiddled, an' Jim Cross called,
The Maiden's Song	22	70	And her dark eyes shone **brigh**,	And her dark eyes shone **bright**, [ES]	And her dark eyes shone **bright**,
The Maiden's Song	30	71	I looked on the beauty her form **bid** embrace,	I looked on the beauty her form **did** embrace, [ES]	I looked on the beauty her form **did** embrace,
My Country Home	7	73	In her yard so calm, **majesic**,	In the yard so calm **majestic**, [MS]	In her yard so calm, **majestic**,
My Country Home	15	73	And **my thoughts** with rapture swelling, Dawns a trodden path to me.	And **my thoughts** with rapture swelling, Dawns a trodden path to me. [MS]	And **[on]** my thoughts, with rapture swelling, Dawns a trodden path to me.
The Foresight	2	75	**Its** nearing day by day;	**It's** nearing day by day; [MS]	**It's** nearing day by day;
The Foresight	8	75	Shall **weal** her trusty sword.	Shall **weal** her trusty sword. [MS]	Shall **wield** her trusty sword.
The Foresight	17	75	And through His precious **promice**,	And through His precious **promise**, [MS]	And through His precious **promise**,
The Foresight	18	75	Like a dark and misty **vail**,	Like a dark and misty **vail**, [MS]	Like a dark and misty **veil**,

EDITING CORRECTIONS

Poem	Line	Page	Original Text	Alternate Text	Corrected Text (This Edition)
The Foresight	30	76	Which **vails** the light before;	Which **vails** the light before, [MS]	Which **veils** the light before,
The Foresight	47	76	Lay **burried** 'neath the waters;	Lay **buried** 'neath the waters; [MS]	Lay **buried** 'neath the waters;
A Congratulation	61	81	Few **fok'es** know de **sutton** fam'ly, [See line 39.]	Few **fo'kes** know de **Sutton** fam'ly, [ES]	Few **fo'kes** know de **Sutton** fam'ly,
The Traveler's Dream	5	82	Full of zeal and of valor, this **travler** had come	Full of zeal and of valor, this **traveler** had come, [MS]	Full of zeal and of valor, this **trav'ler** had come
The Traveler's Dream	13	82	Midst **wreathes** of blossoms and rose.	Midst **wreathes** of blossoms and rose. [MS]	Midst **wreaths** of blossoms and rose.
The Traveler's Dream	32	83	**There** odor and fragrance so sweet.	**Their** odor and fragrance most sweet. [MS]	**Their** odor and fragrance so sweet.
The Traveler's Dream	47	83	In that grim dreary **deapth** through darkness and shade,	In that grim dreary **depth** through darkness and shade, [MS]	In that grim, dreary **depth** through darkness and shade,
The Traveler's Dream	48	83	He beheld an **angle** of death.	He beheld an **angel** of death. [MS]	He beheld an **angel** of death.

EDITING CORRECTIONS

Poem	Line	Page	Original Text	Alternate Text	Corrected Text (This Edition)
The Traveler's Dream	51	83	And the bones on the waste, of that **vail** thick were spread,	And the bones on the waste, of that **vail** thick were spread, [MS]	And the bones on the waste of that **vale** thick were spread,
The Traveler's Dream	58	84	To retrace o'er the route she had **lead**,	He groped for her hand to retrace o'er the route she had **lead**, [MS]	To retrace o'er the route she had **led**;
After the Honeymoon	3	85	Exposein' **mys'f** in the slush an' col'		Exposein' **myse'f** in the slush an' col',
After the Honeymoon	33	86	Exposein' **mys'f** in the slush an' col'		Exposein' **myse'f** in the slush an' col',
After the Honeymoon	55	86	**Hear's** another thing want 'o tell you Miss:		**Here's** another thing want 'o tell you, Miss:
Out Among Um	23	90	**Its** way down old Wes' Seventh Street,		**It's** way down old Wes' Seventh Street,
Out Among Um	24	90	A **spuare** this side o' Brown.		A **square** this side o' Brown.
Out Among Um	32	91	It **Made** me sorter 'fraid.		It **made** me sorter 'fraid.

EDITING CORRECTIONS

Poem	Line	Page	Original Text	Alternate Text	Corrected Text (This Edition)
Our Among Um	75	92	You ought 'o seen us colored **fo'kes,** [See line 15.]		You ought 'o seen us colored **fo'ks**
Our Among Um	113	94	**Atlas'** the big feast ended,		**At las'** the big feast ended,
Quit Yo' Gobblin'!	3	96	Don't you know **its** nigh Thanksgivin'?		Don't you know **it's** nigh Thanksgivin'?
When Johnson's Ban' Comes 'Long	1	97	Come out **hear** boys an' lis'en!		Come out **he'ar** boys an' lis'en!
When Johnson's Ban' Comes 'Long	15	97	The young **fokes** shout an' the ol' turn out, [See line 54.]		The young **fo'ks** shout an' the ol' turn out,
When Johnson's Ban' Comes 'Long	57	98	With years so far **adavnce,**		With years so far **advance;**
When Johnson's Ban' Comes 'Long	59	99	I **be'lieve** she's tryin' to dance.		I **B'lieve** she's tryin' to dance.

EDITING CORRECTIONS

Poem	Line	Page	Original Text	Alternate Text	Corrected Text (This Edition)
When Johnson's Ban' Comes 'Long	75	99	When **e're** his ban' goes by;		When **e'er** his ban' goes by.
When Johnson's Ban' Comes 'Long	81	99	**Its** "Way **down** Dixie Lan'";		**It's** "Way **Down** Dixie Lan'";
A Strange Vision	13	102	And journed **pass** a thousand different worlds,	And journeyed **pass** a thousand different worlds; [ES]	And journeyed **past** a thousand different worlds,
A Strange Vision	17	102	Beheld **tenthousand seraphims** in air,	Beheld **ten thousand seraphim** in air; [ES]	Beheld **ten thousand seraphim** in air;
Invocation	3	104	Lead us, a **trodded** nation, through	Lead us, a **trodden** nation, through [ES]	Lead us, a **trodden** nation, through
Invocation	14	104	Which **vails** the dawning light;	Which **vails** the dawning light; [ES]	Which **veils** the dawning light;

PRISCILLA JANE THOMPSON, *GLEANINGS OF QUIET HOURS*

[EL] = *Ethiope Lays* (1900)

Poem	Line	Page	Original Text	Alternate Text	Corrected Text (This Edition)
Adieu, Adieu, Forever	10	119	**Nomore** the sport of narrow mind I'll be;		**No more** the sport of narrow mind I'll be;

280

EDITING CORRECTIONS

Poem	Line	Page	Original Text	Alternate Text	Corrected Text (This Edition)
Adieu, Adieu, Forever	18	119	My very soul you'd **riflle,**		My very soul you'd **rifle,**
While the Choir Sang	13	124	But there, amongst the aged **saint,**		But there, amongst the aged **saints,**
The Examination	67	133	"Dat's de way you spoke it **to'im,**		"Dat's de way you spoke it **to 'im,**
An Afternoon Gossip	14	144	Jest sit here where **its** cool;		Jest sit here where **it's** cool;
An Afternoon Gossip	101	147	I know 'twa'n't like no **christain,**		I know 'twa'n't like no **christian,**
The Muse's Favor	66	151	Did **paralize** My falt'ring tongue;	Did **paralize** my falt'ring tongue; [EL]	Did **paralyze** My falt'ring tongue;
The Muse's Favor	68	151	That **staid** this song, I sing of thee.	That **staid** this song, I sing of thee. [EL]	That **stayed** this song I sing of thee.
The Favorite Slave's Story	174	158	An' wid a **watchful** eye,		An' wid a **watchful** eye,
The Favorite Slave's Story	197	159	I tell you son, dem **tryin'days,**		I tell you son, dem **tryin' days**

EDITING CORRECTIONS

Poem	Line	Page	Original Text	Alternate Text	Corrected Text (This Edition)
Freedom at McNealy's	34	165	To be **moreof** brute than man;	To be **more of** brute than man; [EL]	To be **more of** brute than man;
After the Quarrel	16	170	When **yon** know, Link's got yo' h'a't. [See line 2.]		When **you** know, Link's got yo' h'a't.
A Little Wren	7	180	Seems half in content and half in **dispair**.		Seems half in content and half in **despair**.
Uncle Jimmie's Yarn	29	188	Den I pulled ole roa'in' **Betsey**, [See line 49.]		Den I pulled ole roa'in' **Betsy**,
Uncle Jimmie's Yarn	37	188	So my fust shot **toe** a slab off;		So my fust shot **to'** a slab off;
Uncle Jimmie's Yarn	65	189	When **atlast** I reached de barracks,		When **at last** I reached de barracks,
Oh, Whence Comes the Gladness?	13	190	The bugbear, the **werwolf**,		The bugbear, the **werewolf**,
The Old Freedman	8	192	Sets him to dreaming as **thou** 'twere night.		Sets him to dreaming as **though** 'twere night.

EDITING CORRECTIONS

Poem	Line	Page	Original Text	Alternate Text	Corrected Text (This Edition)
CLARA ANN THOMPSON, *SONGS FROM THE WAYSIDE*					
Mrs. Johnson Objects	3–4	212	Chasin' aff' them **po'white** children, Jest because you **wan'to** play. [See lines 5 and 17.]		Chasin' aff' them **po' white** children, Jest because you **wan'** to play.
Parted	1	214	She said she **fogave** me; [See line 11.]		She said she **forgave** me;
APPENDIX B: POEMS PUBLISHED IN PERIODICALS					
In Memoriam	5	283	He said "your **war fare** is ended,		He said "your **warfare** is ended,
In Memoriam	6	283	Many **eyes** you have been in the fray;		Many **years** you have been in the fray;
In Memoriam	17	283	**Of** could he return from this journey,		**Or** could he return from this journey,
In Memoriam	22	284	**Gods** plans are all for the best;		**God's** plans are all for the best;
Greetings	6	284	To burdened hearts **being** balms of cheer;		To burdened hearts **bring** balms of cheer;

EDITING CORRECTIONS

Poem	Line	Page	Original Text	Alternate Text	Corrected Text (This Edition)
Chick-O-Ma Craney Crow	11	285	What did it **moan**, does any one know?		What did it **mean**, does any one know?
Chick-O-Ma Craney Crow	13	285	To **me** old school **mate** it seems some how,		To **my** old school **mates** it seems some how,
Little Brown Butterfly	5	286	The roses and bleeding **heart's** beckon to you		The roses and bleeding **hearts** beckon to you

APPENDIX B

Poems Published in Periodicals

AARON BELFORD THOMPSON

In Memoriam
[On the Death of Rev. J.M. Morton]

An Angel came down from the Heavens,
In the tranquil hour of the morn:
He came to the couch where a good Shepherd lay,
In affliction, weary and worn.
He said "your [warfare] is ended,
Many [years] you have been in the fray;
You have fought a good fight, it is finished,
And I come to bear you away.

Away they both journeyed together
To that Sweet Blissful home of the Soul.
The great pearly gateway they entered,
And walked through the streets of pure gold.
Oh could we but see the Heavenly Scenes,
And that Heavenly Music hear;
That the good Shepherd heard through the pearly
    gates,
When he landed safely there.

[Or] could he return from this journey,
In the pulpit once more take his stand;
And tell to his flock in a Heavenly tongue,
The scenes of Sweet Beulah Land.

So weep not friends and dear kindred!
[God's] plans are all for the best;
The shepherd has gone to the kingdom,
To the land where the weary shall rest.

—*The Recorder,* 10 August 1907

Greetings

May peace and plenty e'er remain,
This is my yearning told in rhyme;
Throughout the year let friendship reign,
The same as Merry Christmas Time.
To weary ones lend helping hand,
To burdened hearts [bring] balms of cheer;
Let this resolve spread o'er the land,
From day to day, from year to year.

—*The Recorder,* 23 March 1912

Chick-O-Ma, Craney Crow
From "Rhymes of Childhood"

Chick-o-ma, Chick-oma Craney Crow,
This was the game long ago;
When we were bare-footed boys, you know,
Chick-o-ma, chick-oma craney-crow.

Around, and around, on the same old trail,
Holding each one by his little coat tail;
Forming a laughable childish row,
Chick-o-ma, chick-oma craney-crow.

Though 'twas perplexing to grown up man,
The smallest child could well understand;
What did it [mean], does any one know?
Chick-o-ma, chick-oma craney-crow.

To [my] old school [mates] it seems some how,
We had more fun then than the boys have now;
When we were bare-footed boys, you know,
Chick-o-ma, chick-oma craney-crow.

Since we have all grown to sober faced men,
I often think of the good days then;
Jolly old days of long ago,
Chick-o-ma, chick-oma craney-crow.

—*The Recorder,* 12 February 1927

Color Line

In the silent hour of midnight,
Pondering over things divine,
Came a question, Up in Heaven,
Is there any color line?

Will the holy angels scorn me,
Should the saints invite me in;
Scoff a soul that left a body,
That was wrapped in sable skin?

Then a strange voice broke the silence.
Calm and gentle, soft and low:
Filled my aching heart with gladness,
With a simple answer, "No"!

"There's no hate, no race distinction,
Where the saints and angels dwell;
Color lines are not in Heaven,
Strange to say, they're not in hell."

—*The Chicago Defender,* 4 February 1928

PRISCILLA JANE THOMPSON

Little Brown Butterfly

Little brown Butterfly, artless and gay,
Flitting so airy, from flower to flower,
Come to my garden, just over the way,
Tarry for e'er in my heart's welcome bower,
The roses and bleeding [hearts] beckon to you,
Come, be my valentine now and for aye,
Trifle no more with a heart that is true,
Little brown Butterfly, artless and gay.

—*The Union,* 15 February 1934

APPENDIX C

Complete List of Poems

AARON BELFORD THOMPSON

Key
MS = *Morning Songs* (1899)
ES = *Echoes of Spring* (1901)
HT = *Harvest of Thoughts* (1907)
* = Dialect poem

After the Honeymoon*	HT, *The Freeman*, 12 December 1908
The Bachelor's Soliloquy	ES, HT
A Barnyard Confusion*	HT
Be Ready	MS
Beyond the River	MS, HT
Beyond the Tomb	ES
A Birthday Tribute	MS, HT
Boyhood Days	HT
A Bright Reflection	HT, *The Recorder*, 20 July 1907
The Butterfly	MS
By-Gone Days	ES
Calling	MS
The Chain of Bondage	MS
Chick-O-Ma, Craney Crow	*The Recorder*, 12 February 1927
The Chiming Bells	MS, HT

A Christmas Carol	ES, HT
Color Line	*Chicago Defender,* 4 February 1928
A Congratulation*	ES, HT
Death of Absalom	MS
A Deserted Homestead	ES, HT
Down Murray's Hall*	ES, HT
The Dreary Day	MS, HT
Emancipation	MS, HT
Eulogy on the Farm	ES
Farewell to Summer	MS, HT
The Feast	MS
Fleeting Time	MS
The Foresight	MS, HT
Friendship's Parting	MS, HT
Fritz Mohler's Dream	ES, HT
Goliath and David	MS
Good-Night	ES, HT
Go Ye Unto Every Nation!	MS
Greetings	*The Recorder,* 23 March 1912
I Am Glad	MS
In Memoriam	*The Recorder,* 10 August 1907
Invocation	MS, HT
The Journey of Life	MS
Lead Me	MS, HT
Life's Procession	MS, HT
Lines to Autumn	HT
A Living God	ES
The Lock of Hair	MS
A Lover's Plea	ES
A Love Song	ES
Love's Passion	ES

The Maiden's Song	ES, HT, *The Freeman*, 27 February 1909
A Memorial	ES
A Message	HT
Meum et Tuum	HT, *The Freeman*, 12 December 1908
Midwinter's Reflection	ES
Miss Susie's Social*	ES, HT
A Morning Scene	ES
My Country Home	MS, HT
My Lady Love	ES
My Queen	MS
The Mysteries	ES
New Jerusalem	MS
The New Year	MS
Night	ES, HT, *The Freeman*, 12 December 1908
The Oak Tree	MS
An Ode to Ireland	ES, HT
On the Southern Side	MS
The One I Know	MS
Our Girls	MS, HT
Our National Flag	MS
Out Among Um*	HT
A Plea to the Muse	HT, *The Freeman*, 1 January 1910
A Proposal*	ES, HT
Quit Yo' Gobblin'!*	HT, *The Recorder*, 20 July 1907
Reason Why I's Happy*	HT

A Request	ES
The Rose	ES
The Same Old Sun	MS, HT
Santa Claus' Sleigh Ride	ES, HT
Scenes of Life	MS
The Salf-Same Way	ES
A Serenade	ES, HT
The Shining Star	MS
The Song Bird	MS
A Song to Ethiopia	ES
Spring	ES
A Strange Vision	ES, HT
The Summer Night	MS
Tale of the Haunted Dale	HT
Tale of the Wind	ES, HT
The Tempest	MS
To Helen	ES, HT
The Traveler's Dream	MS, HT
Twilight Hour	ES
Weep Not	HT
What Is Love?	ES
When Johnson's Ban' Comes 'Long*	HT
Work!	MS
Yes	ES

PRISCILLA JANE THOMPSON

Key
EL = *Ethiope Lays* (1900)
GQH = *Gleanings of Quiet Hours* (1907)
* = Dialect poem

Address to Ethiopia	EL, GQH, *The Recorder*, 10 March 1906
Adieu, Adieu, Forever	GQH
Adown the Heights of Ages	GQH
An Afternoon Gossip*	GQH
After the Quarrel*	GQH
Alberta	EL
Athelstane	GQH
Autumn[1]	EL
Autumn[1]	GQH
A Christmas Ghost	GQH
A Common Occurrence*	EL
David and Goliath	EL
Death and Resurrection	GQH
A Domestic Storm*	GQH
Emancipation	GQH
Evelyn	EL
The Examination*	GQH
The Favorite Slave's Story*	GQH
Freedom at McNealy's	EL, GQH
The Fugitive	GQH
Glimpses of Infancy	EL
A Happy Pair	EL

---

[1] These are different poems with the title "Autumn."

A Home Greeting	GQH
The Husband's Return	GQH
A Hymn	EL
The Inner Realm	EL
Insulted*	GQH
The Interrupted Reproof*	GQH
In the Valley	GQH
Just How It Happened*	GQH
A Kindly Deed	GQH
The King's Favorite	EL
Knight of My Maiden Love	EL
Lines on a Dead Girl	EL
Lines to an Old Schoolhouse	GQH
Lines to Emma	GQH
Little Brown Butterfly	*The Union,* 15 February 1934
A Little Wren	GQH
The Muse's Favor	EL, GQH
My Father's Story	EL
Oh, Whence Comes the Gladness?	GQH
The Old Freedman	EL, GQH
The Old Saint's Prayer	EL
The Old Year	GQH
A Prayer	GQH
The Precious Pearl	EL
Raphael	EL, GQH
The Snail's Lesson	EL
The Snow-Flakes	GQH
Soft Black Eyes	GQH
Song of the Moon	GQH
A Southern Scene	EL
They Are the Same	EL
Thwarted	EL
To a Deceased Friend	EL, GQH

To a Little Colored Boy	EL
To the New Year	EL
A Tribute to the Bride and Groom	GQH
The Turn-Coat*	EL, *The Recorder*, 10 March 1906
Uncle Ike's Holiday*	GQH
Uncle Jimmie's Yarn*	GQH
An Unromantic Awakening	EL
A Valentine	GQH
The Vineyard of My Beloved	EL
While the Choir Sang	GQH
A Winter Night	EL

CLARA ANN THOMPSON

Key
SW = *Songs from the Wayside* (1908)
GP = *A Garland of Poems* (1926, Boston: Christopher Publishing)
* = Dialect poem

The After-Glow of Pain	SW
The Angel's Message	SW
Aunt Mandy's Grandchildren*	GP
An Autumn Day	SW
Autumn Leaves	SW
Autumn-Time	GP
Because We Know	GP
Bereavement	GP
Be Sweet	GP
Be True to the Best	GP
The Bonds of Service	GP
But Here by His Side It Is Calm	GP
A Call to Service	GP
Childhood and May	GP
The Christmas Choirs	GP
The Christmas Rush	SW
Church Bells	SW
Circumstantial Evidence	GP
The Common Load	GP
Communion Prayer	GP
Consecration	GP
Conquest	GP
Doubt	SW
Dream Shadows	GP
Drift-wood	SW
The Dying Year	SW

Easter 1919	GP
The Easter Bonnet*	SW
The Easter Light	SW
The Empty Tomb	SW
Faint Heart	GP
The Flirt*	GP
Goin' to Foot It All the Way*	GP
He Comes No More	GP
He Has Always Cared for Me	GP
He Has Bidden Me Go Forward	GP
His Answer	SW
Hope	SW
Hope Deferred	SW
I Dream	GP
If Thou Shouldst Return	SW
I Have Lived for This Hour	GP, *The Union*, 10 December 1921
I'll Follow Thee	SW
In Angel's Guise	GP
Ingrates	GP
Johnny's Pet Superstition*	SW
Let Us Get Back to God	GP
Life and Death	GP
A Lullaby*	SW
Memorial Day	SW
The Minor Key	GP
More Than Ninety Yards	GP
The Mothers Dear	GP
Mrs. Johnson Objects*	SW
The New Schoolhouse	GP
Not Dead, but Sleeping	SW
October	GP
Oh List to My Song!	SW
The Old and the New*	SW

An Opening Service	SW
Our Deceased Leader	GP
Our Heroes	GP, *The Union*, 5 April 1919
Our Idols	GP
Our Side of the Race Problem	GP
Our Soldiers	GP
Out of the Deep	SW
Pap's Advice*	GP
Parted	SW
The Prince of Peace	GP
Raymond G. Dandridge	GP
A Reproof	GP
The Settlement Worker's Prayer	GP
She Prayed	GP
She Sent Him Away	SW
"Showin' Off"*	GP
The Skeptic	SW
Sometime, Somewhere	GP
Spring's Promise	GP
Storm-Beaten	SW
Submission	SW
Temptation	GP
There Came Wise Men	GP
To My Dead Brother	SW
To Obey Is Better Than Sacrifice	GP
Uncle Rube on Church Quarrels*	GP
Uncle Rube on the Race Problem*	SW
Uncle Rube to the Young People*	SW
Uncle Rube's Defense*	SW
The Watcher	SW
What Mean the Bleating of The Sheep?	GP
You'll Have to Come Back to the Road	GP

CPSIA information can be obtained
at www.ICGtesting.com
Printed in the USA
LVHW082103211121
704073LV00003B/20